MSL JOB APPLICATION TRACKING & INTERVIEW SELF-EVALUATION JOURNAL

Copyright © 2024 Dr. Samuel Jacob Dyer • All rights reserved

No part of this content may be reproduced or transmitted for commercial purposes in any form or by any means, electronic or mechanical, including photocopying and recording, or by any data retrieval or storage system information whatsoever, unless authorized in writing by the author.

ISBN: 978-0-9899626-6-7

Published by Medical Science Liaison Inc.

> "The difference between a successful person and others is not a lack of strength, not a lack of knowledge, but rather a lack of will."
>
> — Vince Lombardi

ABOUT THE AUTHOR

Dr. Samuel Dyer is the CEO of the Medical Science Liaison Society and has over 24 years of international MSL experience. During his career, he has managed MSL teams and operations in over 60 countries across the United States, Canada, Europe, Africa, the Middle East, Australia, and New Zealand. He has facilitated the successful launch of pharmaceutical and medical device products for both Fortune 500 pharmaceutical companies and small biotechnology companies.

Dr. Dyer has coached, interviewed, and reviewed the CVs of countless MSL leaders, MSLs and aspiring MSLs. His insights and guidance have resulted in hundreds of aspiring MSLs successfully breaking into their first roles.

While leading the MSL Society, he has conducted MSL training programs for over 65 pharmaceutical, biotechnology, and medical device companies in more than 15 countries. Dr. Dyer has also written extensively on the Medical Science Liaison profession, including numerous published articles, benchmark studies, and reports. He has been the keynote speaker and moderated numerous international conferences on various MSL-related topics, including creating teams, management, MSL training, proper utilization of MSLs, global trends, and the KPIs and metrics used to measure MSL performance. Dr. Dyer has also served as a resource and consultant on a number of MSL-related projects for several organizations, including McKinsey & Company and Bain & Company.

Dr. Dyer has an MD from Washington University (Health & Science) School of Medicine, a PhD in Health Sciences from Touro University, a master's degree in Tropical Biology (where he studied in the Amazon) from Southern Illinois University Edwardsville, and a bachelor's degree in Biology from the University of the State of New York. Dr. Dyer also completed a certificate program for Executive Leadership and Strategy in Pharmaceuticals and Biotechnology at the Harvard Business School.

Dr. Dyer is the author of the multi-award-winning Amazon #1 Best Seller "The Medical Science Liaison Career Guide: How to Break into Your First Role." The book is the first and only step-by-step guide on how to break into the MSL career (www.themslbook.com).

THE IMPORTANCE AND PURPOSE OF THIS JOURNAL

In the ever-changing Medical Science Liaison (MSL) job market, the ability to learn and adapt is crucial. This journal is a customized system for documenting and tracking essential details throughout the application and interview process. Tracking your job applications and interviews provides a structured approach to reflect on successes and areas for improvement.

One of the most useful and unique features of this journal is that it includes 3 comprehensive self-evaluation tools addressing 20 topics critical to success during an MSL interview. This journal also includes a detailed self-evaluation tool addressing 8 topics critical to success during an MSL presentation. All of these self-evaluation tools were developed exclusively for this journal. These tools are invaluable as they provide a structured framework for evaluating your performance, identifying strengths, and pinpointing areas for development. By utilizing these self-evaluation tools, you will gain deeper insights into your interview performance and the ability to refine your strategy for future opportunities.

The diversity of MSL roles and the extensive number of applications and/or interviews that may be necessary can be overwhelming. This journal will serve as your guide, assisting you through the complexities of your job search. Documenting your progress throughout the process also provides valuable self-assessment and insights that can be leveraged to improve your interview skills and techniques. The ability to organize, self-assess, analyze, and learn from each application and/or interview will contribute to your job search success!

HOW TO USE THIS JOURNAL

Tracking the details and organizing the information of multiple job applications and interviews can be overwhelming. This journal is designed to simplify the process and includes 2 separate sections to track both applications and interviews. Begin by filling in the information in the **Application Tracking** section, including the Job Title and Company for each position you have applied for. As you progress, record specific details of each job application, including the application method and login details. Check materials submitted, record the application submission date, note any follow-up actions taken, and track the application status. Because it is likely you will apply to multiple jobs before being invited to an interview, the **Application Tracking** section is designed to track the details of 10 different job applications.

If you are selected for an interview, proceed to the **Interview Tracking** section of the Journal. Begin by filling in the interview details, and capture essential information, including the date, time, and format. In addition, also list the names and titles of those you interview with. Note the specifics of each interview, including how well you did and what can be improved, the questions asked, and your assessment of the responses. Utilize the interview and presentation self-evaluation tools to review your performance, noting areas for improvement. Use the Notes section to record any additional thoughts or insights. It is likely you will interview for several roles before being offered a job. In fact, according to a recent global survey conducted by the Medical Science Liaison Society, 80% of MSLs globally revealed they interviewed with 1-3 companies before being offered their next role. As a result, the **Interview Tracking** section is designed to track the details of 4 different job opportunities.

However, be aware that the MSL interview process typically consists of three rounds of interviews, including a phone screen, phone interview, and in-person interviews. A fourth round of interviews may also be necessary. It's essential to track and capture important details as well as continually self-assess throughout the interview process. As a result, the **Interview Tracking** section is designed to track all of the details for each round of interviews and includes MSL specific self-evaluation tools for each job opportunity.

Consistent use of this journal is essential for maximizing its benefits!

IMPORTANT: Do not bring or complete this workbook during any interview.

APPLICATION TRACKING

MSL JOB APPLICATION TRACKING & INTERVIEW SELF-EVALUATION JOURNAL

JOB OPPORTUNITY
Job Title and Company

Position Applied For:

Therapeutic Area/Disease State/Product:

Geographical Region:

Salary or Salary Range:

Company:

Application Method

☐ Company Website URL: _____

☐ Third-Party Job Board URL: _____

☐ Professional Recruiter: _____

☐ Individual/Networking Contact: _____

Online Application Login Details

Username:

Password:

APPLICATION MATERIALS

☐ CV/Resume   ☐ Cover Letter

APPLICATION SUBMISSION DATE

Date: _____/_____/_____

APPLICATION STATUS
Initial Acknowledgment

☐ Receipt Confirmation and Date:

_____/_____/_____

Follow-Up Actions

Date Sent - Follow-Up Email:

_____/_____/_____

Date Sent - 2nd (final) Follow-Up Email:

_____/_____/_____

Date - Follow-Up Call:

_____/_____/_____

Date - 2nd (final) Follow-Up Call:

_____/_____/_____

Changes in Application Status

☐ Interview Scheduled

☐ Interview Declined

JOB OPPORTUNITY
Job Title and Company

Position Applied For:

Therapeutic Area/Disease State/Product:

Geographical Region:

Salary or Salary Range:

Company:

Application Method

☐ Company Website URL: _____

☐ Third-Party Job Board URL: _____

☐ Professional Recruiter: _____

☐ Individual/Networking Contact: _____

Online Application Login Details

Username:

Password:

APPLICATION MATERIALS

☐ CV/Resume   ☐ Cover Letter

APPLICATION SUBMISSION DATE

Date: _____/_____/_____

APPLICATION STATUS
Initial Acknowledgment

☐ Receipt Confirmation and Date:

_____/_____/_____

Follow-Up Actions

Date Sent - Follow-Up Email:

_____/_____/_____

Date Sent - 2nd (final) Follow-Up Email:

_____/_____/_____

Date - Follow-Up Call:

_____/_____/_____

Date - 2nd (final) Follow-Up Call:

_____/_____/_____

Changes in Application Status

☐ Interview Scheduled

☐ Interview Declined

JOB OPPORTUNITY
Job Title and Company

Position Applied For:

Therapeutic Area/Disease State/Product:

Geographical Region:

Salary or Salary Range:

Company:

Application Method

☐ Company Website URL: _____

☐ Third-Party Job Board URL: _____

☐ Professional Recruiter: _____

☐ Individual/Networking Contact: _____

Online Application Login Details

Username:

Password:

APPLICATION MATERIALS

☐ CV/Resume   ☐ Cover Letter

APPLICATION SUBMISSION DATE

Date: _____/_____/_____

APPLICATION STATUS
Initial Acknowledgment

☐ Receipt Confirmation and Date:

_____/_____/_____

Follow-Up Actions

Date Sent - Follow-Up Email:

_____/_____/_____

Date Sent - 2nd (final) Follow-Up Email:

_____/_____/_____

Date - Follow-Up Call:

_____/_____/_____

Date - 2nd (final) Follow-Up Call:

_____/_____/_____

Changes in Application Status

☐ Interview Scheduled

☐ Interview Declined

MSL JOB APPLICATION TRACKING & INTERVIEW SELF-EVALUATION JOURNAL

JOB OPPORTUNITY
Job Title and Company

Position Applied For:

Therapeutic Area/Disease State/Product:

Geographical Region:

Salary or Salary Range:

Company:

Application Method

☐ Company Website URL: _____

☐ Third-Party Job Board URL: _____

☐ Professional Recruiter: _____

☐ Individual/Networking Contact: _____

Online Application Login Details

Username:

Password:

APPLICATION MATERIALS

☐ CV/Resume   ☐ Cover Letter

APPLICATION SUBMISSION DATE

Date: _____/_____/_____

APPLICATION STATUS
Initial Acknowledgment

☐ Receipt Confirmation and Date:

_____/_____/_____

Follow-Up Actions

Date Sent - Follow-Up Email:

_____/_____/_____

Date Sent - 2nd (final) Follow-Up Email:

_____/_____/_____

Date - Follow-Up Call:

_____/_____/_____

Date - 2nd (final) Follow-Up Call:

_____/_____/_____

Changes in Application Status

☐ Interview Scheduled

☐ Interview Declined

MSL JOB APPLICATION TRACKING & INTERVIEW SELF-EVALUATION JOURNAL

JOB OPPORTUNITY
Job Title and Company

Position Applied For:

Therapeutic Area/Disease State/Product:

Geographical Region:

Salary or Salary Range:

Company:

Application Method

☐ Company Website URL: _____

☐ Third-Party Job Board URL: _____

☐ Professional Recruiter: _____

☐ Individual/Networking Contact: _____

Online Application Login Details

Username:

Password:

APPLICATION MATERIALS

☐ CV/Resume ☐ Cover Letter

APPLICATION SUBMISSION DATE

Date: _____/_____/_____

APPLICATION STATUS
Initial Acknowledgment

☐ Receipt Confirmation and Date:

_____/_____/_____

Follow-Up Actions

Date Sent - Follow-Up Email:
_____/_____/_____

Date Sent - 2nd (final) Follow-Up Email:
_____/_____/_____

Date - Follow-Up Call:
_____/_____/_____

Date - 2nd (final) Follow-Up Call:
_____/_____/_____

Changes in Application Status

☐ Interview Scheduled

☐ Interview Declined

MSL JOB APPLICATION TRACKING & INTERVIEW SELF-EVALUATION JOURNAL

JOB OPPORTUNITY
Job Title and Company

Position Applied For:

Therapeutic Area/Disease State/Product:

Geographical Region:

Salary or Salary Range:

Company:

Application Method

☐ Company Website URL:
_____

☐ Third-Party Job Board URL:
_____

☐ Professional Recruiter:
_____

☐ Individual/Networking Contact:
_____

Online Application Login Details

Username:

Password:

APPLICATION MATERIALS

☐ CV/Resume ☐ Cover Letter

APPLICATION SUBMISSION DATE

Date: _____/_____/_____

APPLICATION STATUS
Initial Acknowledgment

☐ Receipt Confirmation and Date:

_____/_____/_____

Follow-Up Actions

Date Sent - Follow-Up Email:

_____/_____/_____

Date Sent - 2nd (final) Follow-Up Email:

_____/_____/_____

Date - Follow-Up Call:

_____/_____/_____

Date - 2nd (final) Follow-Up Call:

_____/_____/_____

Changes in Application Status

☐ Interview Scheduled

☐ Interview Declined

www.themslbook.com

MSL JOB APPLICATION TRACKING & INTERVIEW SELF-EVALUATION JOURNAL

JOB OPPORTUNITY
Job Title and Company

Position Applied For:

Therapeutic Area/Disease State/Product:

Geographical Region:

Salary or Salary Range:

Company:

Application Method

☐ Company Website URL: _____

☐ Third-Party Job Board URL: _____

☐ Professional Recruiter: _____

☐ Individual/Networking Contact: _____

Online Application Login Details

Username:

Password:

APPLICATION MATERIALS

☐ CV/Resume   ☐ Cover Letter

APPLICATION SUBMISSION DATE

Date: _____/_____/_____

APPLICATION STATUS
Initial Acknowledgment

☐ Receipt Confirmation and Date:

_____/_____/_____

Follow-Up Actions

Date Sent - Follow-Up Email:

_____/_____/_____

Date Sent - 2nd (final) Follow-Up Email:

_____/_____/_____

Date - Follow-Up Call:

_____/_____/_____

Date - 2nd (final) Follow-Up Call:

_____/_____/_____

Changes in Application Status

☐ Interview Scheduled

☐ Interview Declined

MSL JOB APPLICATION TRACKING & INTERVIEW SELF-EVALUATION JOURNAL

JOB OPPORTUNITY
Job Title and Company

Position Applied For:

Therapeutic Area/Disease State/Product:

Geographical Region:

Salary or Salary Range:

Company:

Application Method

☐ Company Website URL: _____

☐ Third-Party Job Board URL: _____

☐ Professional Recruiter: _____

☐ Individual/Networking Contact: _____

Online Application Login Details

Username:

Password:

APPLICATION MATERIALS

☐ CV/Resume   ☐ Cover Letter

APPLICATION SUBMISSION DATE

Date: _____/_____/_____

APPLICATION STATUS
Initial Acknowledgment

☐ Receipt Confirmation and Date:

_____/_____/_____

Follow-Up Actions

Date Sent - Follow-Up Email:

_____/_____/_____

Date Sent - 2nd (final) Follow-Up Email:

_____/_____/_____

Date - Follow-Up Call:

_____/_____/_____

Date - 2nd (final) Follow-Up Call:

_____/_____/_____

Changes in Application Status

☐ Interview Scheduled

☐ Interview Declined

JOB OPPORTUNITY
Job Title and Company

Position Applied For:

Therapeutic Area/Disease State/Product:

Geographical Region:

Salary or Salary Range:

Company:

Application Method

☐ Company Website URL: _____

☐ Third-Party Job Board URL: _____

☐ Professional Recruiter: _____

☐ Individual/Networking Contact: _____

Online Application Login Details

Username:

Password:

APPLICATION MATERIALS

☐ CV/Resume   ☐ Cover Letter

APPLICATION SUBMISSION DATE

Date: _____/_____/_____

APPLICATION STATUS
Initial Acknowledgment

☐ Receipt Confirmation and Date:

_____/_____/_____

Follow-Up Actions

Date Sent - Follow-Up Email:

_____/_____/_____

Date Sent - 2nd (final) Follow-Up Email:

_____/_____/_____

Date - Follow-Up Call:

_____/_____/_____

Date - 2nd (final) Follow-Up Call:

_____/_____/_____

Changes in Application Status

☐ Interview Scheduled

☐ Interview Declined

MSL JOB APPLICATION TRACKING & INTERVIEW SELF-EVALUATION JOURNAL

JOB OPPORTUNITY

Job Title and Company

Position Applied For:

Therapeutic Area/Disease State/Product:

Geographical Region:

Salary or Salary Range:

Company:

Application Method

☐ Company Website URL: _____

☐ Third-Party Job Board URL: _____

☐ Professional Recruiter: _____

☐ Individual/Networking Contact: _____

Online Application Login Details

Username:

Password:

APPLICATION MATERIALS

☐ CV/Resume   ☐ Cover Letter

APPLICATION SUBMISSION DATE

Date: _____/_____/_____

APPLICATION STATUS

Initial Acknowledgment

☐ Receipt Confirmation and Date:

_____/_____/_____

Follow-Up Actions

Date Sent - Follow-Up Email:

_____/_____/_____

Date Sent - 2nd (final) Follow-Up Email:

_____/_____/_____

Date - Follow-Up Call:

_____/_____/_____

Date - 2nd (final) Follow-Up Call:

_____/_____/_____

Changes in Application Status

☐ Interview Scheduled

☐ Interview Declined

INTERVIEW TRACKING

MSL JOB APPLICATION TRACKING & INTERVIEW SELF-EVALUATION JOURNAL

1st INTERVIEW

INTERVIEW DETAILS

Position Applied For: Company:

INTERVIEW DATE, TIME, FORMAT

Scheduled Interview Date: _____/_____/_____

Scheduled Interview Time: _____:_____ ☐ AM ☐ PM

☐ Phone Interview
☐ Virtual Interview
☐ In-Person Interview

Interviewer Details

Names and Titles of Interviewer(s):

1. _____
2. _____
3. _____
4. _____
5. _____
6. _____

What I Did Well

_____
_____
_____
_____

What I Can Improve

_____
_____
_____
_____

MSL JOB APPLICATION TRACKING & INTERVIEW SELF-EVALUATION JOURNAL

1st INTERVIEW

INTERVIEW QUESTIONS

Which questions were most challenging to answer?

1. _____
2. _____
3. _____
4. _____

Key questions you were asked:

1. _____
2. _____
3. _____
4. _____

Self-assessment of my responses:

1. _____
2. _____
3. _____
4. _____

MSL JOB APPLICATION TRACKING & INTERVIEW SELF-EVALUATION JOURNAL

INTERVIEW SELF-EVALUATION

1st INTERVIEW

	Strongly Agree	Agree	Neutral	Disagree	Strongly Disagree	Not Applicable
Disease State / Therapeutic Area Expertise: I effectively communicated my expertise in the specific disease state and therapeutic area relevant to the role.	☐	☐	☐	☐	☐	☐
KOL Engagement: I effectively communicated my experience engaging Key Opinion Leaders (KOLs) and Health Care Providers (HCPs).	☐	☐	☐	☐	☐	☐
Product Knowledge: I demonstrated a deep understanding of the company's products and their clinical applications.	☐	☐	☐	☐	☐	☐
Clinical Trial Knowledge: I demonstrated a solid understanding of clinical trial methodologies and their relevance.	☐	☐	☐	☐	☐	☐
Regulatory/Compliance Knowledge: I highlighted knowledge of regulatory guidelines and compliance standards relevant to the role.	☐	☐	☐	☐	☐	☐
Relationship Building: I highlighted my experience in building and maintaining professional relationships both internally and externally.	☐	☐	☐	☐	☐	☐

INTERVIEW SELF-EVALUATION

1st INTERVIEW

	Strongly Agree	Agree	Neutral	Disagree	Strongly Disagree	Not Applicable
Coachability: I demonstrated an openness to feedback and a willingness to incorporate suggestions provided by colleagues and management.	☐	☐	☐	☐	☐	☐
Clinical Data Interpretation: I demonstrated the ability to interpret and discuss clinical data effectively.	☐	☐	☐	☐	☐	☐
Flexibility: I demonstrated flexibility and adaptability in responding to unexpected questions or situations.	☐	☐	☐	☐	☐	☐
Overall Confidence: I felt confident and poised throughout the interview.	☐	☐	☐	☐	☐	☐
Handling Challenging Questions: I effectively navigated and responded to challenging or unexpected questions during the interview.	☐	☐	☐	☐	☐	☐
Succinct Responses to Interview Questions: I responded succinctly to interview questions, providing clear and concise answers without unnecessary elaboration.	☐	☐	☐	☐	☐	☐
Competitor Knowledge: I demonstrated knowledge of the competitive landscape and effectively communicated distinctions between the company's products and its competitors.	☐	☐	☐	☐	☐	☐

INTERVIEW SELF-EVALUATION

1st INTERVIEW

	Strongly Agree	Agree	Neutral	Disagree	Strongly Disagree	Not Applicable
Strategic Thinking: I demonstrated strategic thinking in discussing how the company's products fit into the broader healthcare landscape.	☐	☐	☐	☐	☐	☐
Digital Communication Skills: I effectively conveyed my proficiency in utilizing digital communication tools for scientific engagement.	☐	☐	☐	☐	☐	☐
Continual Learning: I highlighted my commitment to continual learning and staying updated on advancements in the therapeutic area.	☐	☐	☐	☐	☐	☐
Team Collaboration: I emphasized my ability to collaborate effectively with team members and cross-functional teams.	☐	☐	☐	☐	☐	☐
Enthusiasm for the Role: I effectively conveyed genuine enthusiasm for the role and the science of the product.	☐	☐	☐	☐	☐	☐
Asking Relevant Questions: I proactively asked relevant questions during the interview, demonstrating a genuine interest and understanding of the role.	☐	☐	☐	☐	☐	☐
STAR Method Application: When expected, I effectively utilized the STAR (Situation, Task, Action, Result) method when responding to behavioral questions.	☐	☐	☐	☐	☐	☐

MSL JOB APPLICATION TRACKING & INTERVIEW SELF-EVALUATION JOURNAL

1st INTERVIEW

PRESENTATION SELF-EVALUATION*

	Strongly Agree	Agree	Neutral	Disagree	Strongly Disagree
Clarity of Message: I clearly and effectively communicated the key points of my presentation.	☐	☐	☐	☐	☐
Engagement with Audience: I maintained audience engagement by using effective visuals, body language, and vocal tone.	☐	☐	☐	☐	☐
Knowledge Demonstration: I demonstrated a comprehensive understanding of the subject matter and responded confidently to questions.	☐	☐	☐	☐	☐
Visual Aids Effectiveness: The visual aids (slides, charts, etc.) I utilized enhanced the overall impact of my presentation.	☐	☐	☐	☐	☐
Time Management: I effectively utilized the allotted time, ensuring all key points were covered within the specified timeframe.	☐	☐	☐	☐	☐
Adaptability to Audience: I adapted my presentation style to suit the needs and level of understanding of the audience.	☐	☐	☐	☐	☐
Overall Confidence: I felt confident and poised throughout the presentation.	☐	☐	☐	☐	☐
Communicating Scientific Information: I demonstrated strong presentation skills in conveying scientific information to a diverse audience.	☐	☐	☐	☐	☐

*Although most applicants will be expected to deliver a presentation once during the interview process (typically during the in-person interview), it's important to be prepared to present at any point throughout the process.

MSL JOB APPLICATION TRACKING & INTERVIEW SELF-EVALUATION JOURNAL

1st INTERVIEW

THANK-YOU LETTER

Date Sent: _____/_____/_____

Individual's Name:

Email Address:

NOTES

_____
_____
_____
_____
_____
_____
_____
_____
_____
_____
_____

MSL JOB APPLICATION TRACKING & INTERVIEW SELF-EVALUATION JOURNAL

2nd INTERVIEW

INTERVIEW DETAILS

Position Applied For:　　　　　　　　　　　Company:

INTERVIEW DATE, TIME, FORMAT

Scheduled Interview Date: _____/_____/_____

Scheduled Interview Time: _____:_____ ☐ AM ☐ PM

☐ Phone Interview
☐ Virtual Interview
☐ In-Person Interview

Interviewer Details

Names and Titles of Interviewer(s):

1. _____
2. _____
3. _____
4. _____
5. _____
6. _____

What I Did Well

_____
_____
_____
_____
_____

What I Can Improve

_____
_____
_____
_____
_____

MSL JOB APPLICATION TRACKING & INTERVIEW SELF-EVALUATION JOURNAL

2nd INTERVIEW

INTERVIEW QUESTIONS

Which questions were most challenging to answer?

1. _____
2. _____
3. _____
4. _____

Key questions you were asked:

1. _____
2. _____
3. _____
4. _____

Self-assessment of my responses:

1. _____
2. _____
3. _____
4. _____

INTERVIEW SELF-EVALUATION

	Strongly Agree	Agree	Neutral	Disagree	Strongly Disagree	Not Applicable
Disease State / Therapeutic Area Expertise: I effectively communicated my expertise in the specific disease state and therapeutic area relevant to the role.	☐	☐	☐	☐	☐	☐
KOL Engagement: I effectively communicated my experience engaging Key Opinion Leaders (KOLs) and Health Care Providers (HCPs).	☐	☐	☐	☐	☐	☐
Product Knowledge: I demonstrated a deep understanding of the company's products and their clinical applications.	☐	☐	☐	☐	☐	☐
Clinical Trial Knowledge: I demonstrated a solid understanding of clinical trial methodologies and their relevance.	☐	☐	☐	☐	☐	☐
Regulatory/Compliance Knowledge: I highlighted knowledge of regulatory guidelines and compliance standards relevant to the role.	☐	☐	☐	☐	☐	☐
Relationship Building: I highlighted my experience in building and maintaining professional relationships both internally and externally.	☐	☐	☐	☐	☐	☐

INTERVIEW SELF-EVALUATION

2nd INTERVIEW

	Strongly Agree	Agree	Neutral	Disagree	Strongly Disagree	Not Applicable
Coachability: I demonstrated an openness to feedback and a willingness to incorporate suggestions provided by colleagues and management.	☐	☐	☐	☐	☐	☐
Clinical Data Interpretation: I demonstrated the ability to interpret and discuss clinical data effectively.	☐	☐	☐	☐	☐	☐
Flexibility: I demonstrated flexibility and adaptability in responding to unexpected questions or situations.	☐	☐	☐	☐	☐	☐
Overall Confidence: I felt confident and poised throughout the interview.	☐	☐	☐	☐	☐	☐
Handling Challenging Questions: I effectively navigated and responded to challenging or unexpected questions during the interview.	☐	☐	☐	☐	☐	☐
Succinct Responses to Interview Questions: I responded succinctly to interview questions, providing clear and concise answers without unnecessary elaboration.	☐	☐	☐	☐	☐	☐
Competitor Knowledge: I demonstrated knowledge of the competitive landscape and effectively communicated distinctions between the company's products and its competitors.	☐	☐	☐	☐	☐	☐

MSL JOB APPLICATION TRACKING & INTERVIEW SELF-EVALUATION JOURNAL

2nd INTERVIEW

INTERVIEW SELF-EVALUATION

	Strongly Agree	Agree	Neutral	Disagree	Strongly Disagree	Not Applicable
Strategic Thinking: I demonstrated strategic thinking in discussing how the company's products fit into the broader healthcare landscape.	☐	☐	☐	☐	☐	☐
Digital Communication Skills: I effectively conveyed my proficiency in utilizing digital communication tools for scientific engagement.	☐	☐	☐	☐	☐	☐
Continual Learning: I highlighted my commitment to continual learning and staying updated on advancements in the therapeutic area.	☐	☐	☐	☐	☐	☐
Team Collaboration: I emphasized my ability to collaborate effectively with team members and cross-functional teams.	☐	☐	☐	☐	☐	☐
Enthusiasm for the Role: I effectively conveyed genuine enthusiasm for the role and the science of the product.	☐	☐	☐	☐	☐	☐
Asking Relevant Questions: I proactively asked relevant questions during the interview, demonstrating a genuine interest and understanding of the role.	☐	☐	☐	☐	☐	☐
STAR Method Application: When expected, I effectively utilized the STAR (Situation, Task, Action, Result) method when responding to behavioral questions.	☐	☐	☐	☐	☐	☐

MSL JOB APPLICATION TRACKING & INTERVIEW SELF-EVALUATION JOURNAL

2nd INTERVIEW

PRESENTATION SELF-EVALUATION*

	Strongly Agree	Agree	Neutral	Disagree	Strongly Disagree
Clarity of Message: I clearly and effectively communicated the key points of my presentation.	☐	☐	☐	☐	☐
Engagement with Audience: I maintained audience engagement by using effective visuals, body language, and vocal tone.	☐	☐	☐	☐	☐
Knowledge Demonstration: I demonstrated a comprehensive understanding of the subject matter and responded confidently to questions.	☐	☐	☐	☐	☐
Visual Aids Effectiveness: The visual aids (slides, charts, etc.) I utilized enhanced the overall impact of my presentation.	☐	☐	☐	☐	☐
Time Management: I effectively utilized the allotted time, ensuring all key points were covered within the specified timeframe.	☐	☐	☐	☐	☐
Adaptability to Audience: I adapted my presentation style to suit the needs and level of understanding of the audience.	☐	☐	☐	☐	☐
Overall Confidence: I felt confident and poised throughout the presentation.	☐	☐	☐	☐	☐
Communicating Scientific Information: I demonstrated strong presentation skills in conveying scientific information to a diverse audience.	☐	☐	☐	☐	☐

*Although most applicants will be expected to deliver a presentation once during the interview process (typically during the in-person interview), it's important to be prepared to present at any point throughout the process.

MSL JOB APPLICATION TRACKING & INTERVIEW SELF-EVALUATION JOURNAL

2nd INTERVIEW

THANK-YOU LETTER

Date Sent: _____/_____/_____

Individual's Name:

Email Address:

NOTES

_____
_____
_____
_____
_____
_____
_____
_____
_____
_____
_____

MSL JOB APPLICATION TRACKING & INTERVIEW SELF-EVALUATION JOURNAL

3rd INTERVIEW

INTERVIEW DETAILS

Position Applied For: Company:

INTERVIEW DATE, TIME, FORMAT

Scheduled Interview Date: _____ / _____ / _____

Scheduled Interview Time: ____ : ____ ☐ AM ☐ PM

☐ Phone Interview
☐ Virtual Interview
☐ In-Person Interview

Interviewer Details

Names and Titles of Interviewer(s):

1. _____
2. _____
3. _____
4. _____
5. _____
6. _____

What I Did Well

_____

_____

_____

_____

What I Can Improve

_____

_____

_____

_____

MSL JOB APPLICATION TRACKING & INTERVIEW SELF-EVALUATION JOURNAL

3rd INTERVIEW

INTERVIEW QUESTIONS

Which questions were most challenging to answer?

1. _____
2. _____
3. _____
4. _____

Key questions you were asked:

1. _____
2. _____
3. _____
4. _____

Self-assessment of my responses:

1. _____
2. _____
3. _____
4. _____

MSL JOB APPLICATION TRACKING & INTERVIEW SELF-EVALUATION JOURNAL

3rd INTERVIEW

INTERVIEW SELF-EVALUATION

	Strongly Agree	Agree	Neutral	Disagree	Strongly Disagree	Not Applicable
Disease State / Therapeutic Area Expertise: I effectively communicated my expertise in the specific disease state and therapeutic area relevant to the role.	☐	☐	☐	☐	☐	☐
KOL Engagement: I effectively communicated my experience engaging Key Opinion Leaders (KOLs) and Health Care Providers (HCPs).	☐	☐	☐	☐	☐	☐
Product Knowledge: I demonstrated a deep understanding of the company's products and their clinical applications.	☐	☐	☐	☐	☐	☐
Clinical Trial Knowledge: I demonstrated a solid understanding of clinical trial methodologies and their relevance.	☐	☐	☐	☐	☐	☐
Regulatory/Compliance Knowledge: I highlighted knowledge of regulatory guidelines and compliance standards relevant to the role.	☐	☐	☐	☐	☐	☐
Relationship Building: I highlighted my experience in building and maintaining professional relationships both internally and externally.	☐	☐	☐	☐	☐	☐

www.themslbook.com

MSL JOB APPLICATION TRACKING & INTERVIEW SELF-EVALUATION JOURNAL

INTERVIEW SELF-EVALUATION

3rd INTERVIEW

	Strongly Agree	Agree	Neutral	Disagree	Strongly Disagree	Not Applicable
Coachability: I demonstrated an openness to feedback and a willingness to incorporate suggestions provided by colleagues and management.	☐	☐	☐	☐	☐	☐
Clinical Data Interpretation: I demonstrated the ability to interpret and discuss clinical data effectively.	☐	☐	☐	☐	☐	☐
Flexibility: I demonstrated flexibility and adaptability in responding to unexpected questions or situations.	☐	☐	☐	☐	☐	☐
Overall Confidence: I felt confident and poised throughout the interview.	☐	☐	☐	☐	☐	☐
Handling Challenging Questions: I effectively navigated and responded to challenging or unexpected questions during the interview.	☐	☐	☐	☐	☐	☐
Succinct Responses to Interview Questions: I responded succinctly to interview questions, providing clear and concise answers without unnecessary elaboration.	☐	☐	☐	☐	☐	☐
Competitor Knowledge: I demonstrated knowledge of the competitive landscape and effectively communicated distinctions between the company's products and its competitors.	☐	☐	☐	☐	☐	☐

MSL JOB APPLICATION TRACKING & INTERVIEW SELF-EVALUATION JOURNAL

3rd INTERVIEW

INTERVIEW SELF-EVALUATION

	Strongly Agree	Agree	Neutral	Disagree	Strongly Disagree	Not Applicable
Strategic Thinking: I demonstrated strategic thinking in discussing how the company's products fit into the broader healthcare landscape.	☐	☐	☐	☐	☐	☐
Digital Communication Skills: I effectively conveyed my proficiency in utilizing digital communication tools for scientific engagement.	☐	☐	☐	☐	☐	☐
Continual Learning: I highlighted my commitment to continual learning and staying updated on advancements in the therapeutic area.	☐	☐	☐	☐	☐	☐
Team Collaboration: I emphasized my ability to collaborate effectively with team members and cross-functional teams.	☐	☐	☐	☐	☐	☐
Enthusiasm for the Role: I effectively conveyed genuine enthusiasm for the role and the science of the product.	☐	☐	☐	☐	☐	☐
Asking Relevant Questions: I proactively asked relevant questions during the interview, demonstrating a genuine interest and understanding of the role.	☐	☐	☐	☐	☐	☐
STAR Method Application: When expected, I effectively utilized the STAR (Situation, Task, Action, Result) method when responding to behavioral questions.	☐	☐	☐	☐	☐	☐

MSL JOB APPLICATION TRACKING & INTERVIEW SELF-EVALUATION JOURNAL

3rd INTERVIEW

PRESENTATION SELF-EVALUATION*

	Strongly Agree	Agree	Neutral	Disagree	Strongly Disagree
Clarity of Message: I clearly and effectively communicated the key points of my presentation.	☐	☐	☐	☐	☐
Engagement with Audience: I maintained audience engagement by using effective visuals, body language, and vocal tone.	☐	☐	☐	☐	☐
Knowledge Demonstration: I demonstrated a comprehensive understanding of the subject matter and responded confidently to questions.	☐	☐	☐	☐	☐
Visual Aids Effectiveness: The visual aids (slides, charts, etc.) I utilized enhanced the overall impact of my presentation.	☐	☐	☐	☐	☐
Time Management: I effectively utilized the allotted time, ensuring all key points were covered within the specified timeframe.	☐	☐	☐	☐	☐
Adaptability to Audience: I adapted my presentation style to suit the needs and level of understanding of the audience.	☐	☐	☐	☐	☐
Overall Confidence: I felt confident and poised throughout the presentation.	☐	☐	☐	☐	☐
Communicating Scientific Information: I demonstrated strong presentation skills in conveying scientific information to a diverse audience.	☐	☐	☐	☐	☐

*Although most applicants will be expected to deliver a presentation once during the interview process (typically during the in-person interview), it's important to be prepared to present at any point throughout the process.

MSL JOB APPLICATION TRACKING & INTERVIEW SELF-EVALUATION JOURNAL

3rd
INTERVIEW

THANK-YOU LETTER

Date Sent: _____/_____/_____

Individual's Name:

Email Address:

NOTES

_____
_____
_____
_____
_____
_____
_____
_____
_____
_____
_____
_____

MSL JOB APPLICATION TRACKING & INTERVIEW SELF-EVALUATION JOURNAL

4th INTERVIEW

INTERVIEW DETAILS

Position Applied For: _____   Company: _____

INTERVIEW DATE, TIME, FORMAT

Scheduled Interview Date: _____/_____/_____

Scheduled Interview Time: _____ : _____ ☐ AM ☐ PM

☐ Phone Interview
☐ Virtual Interview
☐ In-Person Interview

Interviewer Details

Names and Titles of Interviewer(s):

1. _____
2. _____
3. _____
4. _____
5. _____
6. _____

What I Did Well

_____
_____
_____
_____
_____

What I Can Improve

_____
_____
_____
_____
_____

MSL JOB APPLICATION TRACKING & INTERVIEW SELF-EVALUATION JOURNAL

4th INTERVIEW

INTERVIEW QUESTIONS

Which questions were most challenging to answer?

1. _____
2. _____
3. _____
4. _____

Key questions you were asked:

1. _____
2. _____
3. _____
4. _____

Self-assessment of my responses:

1. _____
2. _____
3. _____
4. _____

MSL JOB APPLICATION TRACKING & INTERVIEW SELF-EVALUATION JOURNAL

4th INTERVIEW

INTERVIEW SELF-EVALUATION

	Strongly Agree	Agree	Neutral	Disagree	Strongly Disagree	Not Applicable
Disease State / Therapeutic Area Expertise: I effectively communicated my expertise in the specific disease state and therapeutic area relevant to the role.	☐	☐	☐	☐	☐	☐
KOL Engagement: I effectively communicated my experience engaging Key Opinion Leaders (KOLs) and Health Care Providers (HCPs).	☐	☐	☐	☐	☐	☐
Product Knowledge: I demonstrated a deep understanding of the company's products and their clinical applications.	☐	☐	☐	☐	☐	☐
Clinical Trial Knowledge: I demonstrated a solid understanding of clinical trial methodologies and their relevance.	☐	☐	☐	☐	☐	☐
Regulatory/Compliance Knowledge: I highlighted knowledge of regulatory guidelines and compliance standards relevant to the role.	☐	☐	☐	☐	☐	☐
Relationship Building: I highlighted my experience in building and maintaining professional relationships both internally and externally.	☐	☐	☐	☐	☐	☐

MSL JOB APPLICATION TRACKING & INTERVIEW SELF-EVALUATION JOURNAL

INTERVIEW SELF-EVALUATION

4th INTERVIEW

	Strongly Agree	Agree	Neutral	Disagree	Strongly Disagree	Not Applicable
Coachability: I demonstrated an openness to feedback and a willingness to incorporate suggestions provided by colleagues and management.	☐	☐	☐	☐	☐	☐
Clinical Data Interpretation: I demonstrated the ability to interpret and discuss clinical data effectively.	☐	☐	☐	☐	☐	☐
Flexibility: I demonstrated flexibility and adaptability in responding to unexpected questions or situations.	☐	☐	☐	☐	☐	☐
Overall Confidence: I felt confident and poised throughout the interview.	☐	☐	☐	☐	☐	☐
Handling Challenging Questions: I effectively navigated and responded to challenging or unexpected questions during the interview.	☐	☐	☐	☐	☐	☐
Succinct Responses to Interview Questions: I responded succinctly to interview questions, providing clear and concise answers without unnecessary elaboration.	☐	☐	☐	☐	☐	☐
Competitor Knowledge: I demonstrated knowledge of the competitive landscape and effectively communicated distinctions between the company's products and its competitors.	☐	☐	☐	☐	☐	☐

INTERVIEW SELF-EVALUATION

4th INTERVIEW

	Strongly Agree	Agree	Neutral	Disagree	Strongly Disagree	Not Applicable
Strategic Thinking: I demonstrated strategic thinking in discussing how the company's products fit into the broader healthcare landscape.	☐	☐	☐	☐	☐	☐
Digital Communication Skills: I effectively conveyed my proficiency in utilizing digital communication tools for scientific engagement.	☐	☐	☐	☐	☐	☐
Continual Learning: I highlighted my commitment to continual learning and staying updated on advancements in the therapeutic area.	☐	☐	☐	☐	☐	☐
Team Collaboration: I emphasized my ability to collaborate effectively with team members and cross-functional teams.	☐	☐	☐	☐	☐	☐
Enthusiasm for the Role: I effectively conveyed genuine enthusiasm for the role and the science of the product.	☐	☐	☐	☐	☐	☐
Asking Relevant Questions: I proactively asked relevant questions during the interview, demonstrating a genuine interest and understanding of the role.	☐	☐	☐	☐	☐	☐
STAR Method Application: When expected, I effectively utilized the STAR (Situation, Task, Action, Result) method when responding to behavioral questions.	☐	☐	☐	☐	☐	☐

MSL JOB APPLICATION TRACKING & INTERVIEW SELF-EVALUATION JOURNAL

4th INTERVIEW

PRESENTATION SELF-EVALUATION*

	Strongly Agree	Agree	Neutral	Disagree	Strongly Disagree
Clarity of Message: I clearly and effectively communicated the key points of my presentation.	☐	☐	☐	☐	☐
Engagement with Audience: I maintained audience engagement by using effective visuals, body language, and vocal tone.	☐	☐	☐	☐	☐
Knowledge Demonstration: I demonstrated a comprehensive understanding of the subject matter and responded confidently to questions.	☐	☐	☐	☐	☐
Visual Aids Effectiveness: The visual aids (slides, charts, etc.) I utilized enhanced the overall impact of my presentation.	☐	☐	☐	☐	☐
Time Management: I effectively utilized the allotted time, ensuring all key points were covered within the specified timeframe.	☐	☐	☐	☐	☐
Adaptability to Audience: I adapted my presentation style to suit the needs and level of understanding of the audience.	☐	☐	☐	☐	☐
Overall Confidence: I felt confident and poised throughout the presentation.	☐	☐	☐	☐	☐
Communicating Scientific Information: I demonstrated strong presentation skills in conveying scientific information to a diverse audience.	☐	☐	☐	☐	☐

*Although most applicants will be expected to deliver a presentation once during the interview process (typically during the in-person interview), it's important to be prepared to present at any point throughout the process.

www.themslbook.com

MSL JOB APPLICATION TRACKING & INTERVIEW SELF-EVALUATION JOURNAL

4th INTERVIEW

THANK-YOU LETTER

Date Sent: _____/_____/_____

Individual's Name:

Email Address:

NOTES

_____
_____
_____
_____
_____
_____
_____
_____
_____
_____

INTERVIEW TRACKING

MSL JOB APPLICATION TRACKING & INTERVIEW SELF-EVALUATION JOURNAL

1st INTERVIEW

INTERVIEW DETAILS

Position Applied For: _____   Company: _____

INTERVIEW DATE, TIME, FORMAT

Scheduled Interview Date: _____/_____/_____

Scheduled Interview Time: ____:____ ☐ AM ☐ PM

☐ Phone Interview
☐ Virtual Interview
☐ In-Person Interview

Interviewer Details

Names and Titles of Interviewer(s):

1. _____   4. _____

2. _____   5. _____

3. _____   6. _____

What I Did Well

_____
_____
_____
_____

What I Can Improve

_____
_____
_____
_____

MSL JOB APPLICATION TRACKING & INTERVIEW SELF-EVALUATION JOURNAL

1st INTERVIEW

INTERVIEW QUESTIONS

Which questions were most challenging to answer?

1. _____
2. _____
3. _____
4. _____

Key questions you were asked:

1. _____
2. _____
3. _____
4. _____

Self-assessment of my responses:

1. _____
2. _____
3. _____
4. _____

MSL JOB APPLICATION TRACKING & INTERVIEW SELF-EVALUATION JOURNAL

INTERVIEW SELF-EVALUATION

1st INTERVIEW

	Strongly Agree	Agree	Neutral	Disagree	Strongly Disagree	Not Applicable
Disease State / Therapeutic Area Expertise: I effectively communicated my expertise in the specific disease state and therapeutic area relevant to the role.	☐	☐	☐	☐	☐	☐
KOL Engagement: I effectively communicated my experience engaging Key Opinion Leaders (KOLs) and Health Care Providers (HCPs).	☐	☐	☐	☐	☐	☐
Product Knowledge: I demonstrated a deep understanding of the company's products and their clinical applications.	☐	☐	☐	☐	☐	☐
Clinical Trial Knowledge: I demonstrated a solid understanding of clinical trial methodologies and their relevance.	☐	☐	☐	☐	☐	☐
Regulatory/Compliance Knowledge: I highlighted knowledge of regulatory guidelines and compliance standards relevant to the role.	☐	☐	☐	☐	☐	☐
Relationship Building: I highlighted my experience in building and maintaining professional relationships both internally and externally.	☐	☐	☐	☐	☐	☐

INTERVIEW SELF-EVALUATION

1st INTERVIEW

	Strongly Agree	Agree	Neutral	Disagree	Strongly Disagree	Not Applicable
Coachability: I demonstrated an openness to feedback and a willingness to incorporate suggestions provided by colleagues and management.	☐	☐	☐	☐	☐	☐
Clinical Data Interpretation: I demonstrated the ability to interpret and discuss clinical data effectively.	☐	☐	☐	☐	☐	☐
Flexibility: I demonstrated flexibility and adaptability in responding to unexpected questions or situations.	☐	☐	☐	☐	☐	☐
Overall Confidence: I felt confident and poised throughout the interview.	☐	☐	☐	☐	☐	☐
Handling Challenging Questions: I effectively navigated and responded to challenging or unexpected questions during the interview.	☐	☐	☐	☐	☐	☐
Succinct Responses to Interview Questions: I responded succinctly to interview questions, providing clear and concise answers without unnecessary elaboration.	☐	☐	☐	☐	☐	☐
Competitor Knowledge: I demonstrated knowledge of the competitive landscape and effectively communicated distinctions between the company's products and its competitors.	☐	☐	☐	☐	☐	☐

INTERVIEW SELF-EVALUATION

1st INTERVIEW

	Strongly Agree	Agree	Neutral	Disagree	Strongly Disagree	Not Applicable
Strategic Thinking: I demonstrated strategic thinking in discussing how the company's products fit into the broader healthcare landscape.	☐	☐	☐	☐	☐	☐
Digital Communication Skills: I effectively conveyed my proficiency in utilizing digital communication tools for scientific engagement.	☐	☐	☐	☐	☐	☐
Continual Learning: I highlighted my commitment to continual learning and staying updated on advancements in the therapeutic area.	☐	☐	☐	☐	☐	☐
Team Collaboration: I emphasized my ability to collaborate effectively with team members and cross-functional teams.	☐	☐	☐	☐	☐	☐
Enthusiasm for the Role: I effectively conveyed genuine enthusiasm for the role and the science of the product.	☐	☐	☐	☐	☐	☐
Asking Relevant Questions: I proactively asked relevant questions during the interview, demonstrating a genuine interest and understanding of the role.	☐	☐	☐	☐	☐	☐
STAR Method Application: When expected, I effectively utilized the STAR (Situation, Task, Action, Result) method when responding to behavioral questions.	☐	☐	☐	☐	☐	☐

PRESENTATION SELF-EVALUATION*

	Strongly Agree	Agree	Neutral	Disagree	Strongly Disagree
Clarity of Message: I clearly and effectively communicated the key points of my presentation.	☐	☐	☐	☐	☐
Engagement with Audience: I maintained audience engagement by using effective visuals, body language, and vocal tone.	☐	☐	☐	☐	☐
Knowledge Demonstration: I demonstrated a comprehensive understanding of the subject matter and responded confidently to questions.	☐	☐	☐	☐	☐
Visual Aids Effectiveness: The visual aids (slides, charts, etc.) I utilized enhanced the overall impact of my presentation.	☐	☐	☐	☐	☐
Time Management: I effectively utilized the allotted time, ensuring all key points were covered within the specified timeframe.	☐	☐	☐	☐	☐
Adaptability to Audience: I adapted my presentation style to suit the needs and level of understanding of the audience.	☐	☐	☐	☐	☐
Overall Confidence: I felt confident and poised throughout the presentation.	☐	☐	☐	☐	☐
Communicating Scientific Information: I demonstrated strong presentation skills in conveying scientific information to a diverse audience.	☐	☐	☐	☐	☐

*Although most applicants will be expected to deliver a presentation once during the interview process (typically during the in-person interview), it's important to be prepared to present at any point throughout the process.

THANK-YOU LETTER

Date Sent: _____/_____/_____

Individual's Name:

Email Address:

NOTES

_____
_____
_____
_____
_____
_____
_____
_____
_____
_____
_____
_____

1st INTERVIEW

MSL JOB APPLICATION TRACKING & INTERVIEW SELF-EVALUATION JOURNAL

2nd INTERVIEW

INTERVIEW DETAILS

Position Applied For: _____ Company: _____

INTERVIEW DATE, TIME, FORMAT

Scheduled Interview Date: _____ / _____ / _____

Scheduled Interview Time: _____ : _____ ☐ AM ☐ PM

☐ Phone Interview
☐ Virtual Interview
☐ In-Person Interview

Interviewer Details

Names and Titles of Interviewer(s):

1. _____
2. _____
3. _____
4. _____
5. _____
6. _____

What I Did Well

_____
_____
_____
_____

What I Can Improve

_____
_____
_____
_____

MSL JOB APPLICATION TRACKING & INTERVIEW SELF-EVALUATION JOURNAL

2nd INTERVIEW

INTERVIEW QUESTIONS

Which questions were most challenging to answer?

1. _____
2. _____
3. _____
4. _____

Key questions you were asked:

1. _____
2. _____
3. _____
4. _____

Self-assessment of my responses:

1. _____
2. _____
3. _____
4. _____

MSL JOB APPLICATION TRACKING & INTERVIEW SELF-EVALUATION JOURNAL

INTERVIEW SELF-EVALUATION

2nd INTERVIEW

	Strongly Agree	Agree	Neutral	Disagree	Strongly Disagree	Not Applicable
Disease State / Therapeutic Area Expertise: I effectively communicated my expertise in the specific disease state and therapeutic area relevant to the role.	☐	☐	☐	☐	☐	☐
KOL Engagement: I effectively communicated my experience engaging Key Opinion Leaders (KOLs) and Health Care Providers (HCPs).	☐	☐	☐	☐	☐	☐
Product Knowledge: I demonstrated a deep understanding of the company's products and their clinical applications.	☐	☐	☐	☐	☐	☐
Clinical Trial Knowledge: I demonstrated a solid understanding of clinical trial methodologies and their relevance.	☐	☐	☐	☐	☐	☐
Regulatory/Compliance Knowledge: I highlighted knowledge of regulatory guidelines and compliance standards relevant to the role.	☐	☐	☐	☐	☐	☐
Relationship Building: I highlighted my experience in building and maintaining professional relationships both internally and externally.	☐	☐	☐	☐	☐	☐

MSL JOB APPLICATION TRACKING & INTERVIEW SELF-EVALUATION JOURNAL

2nd INTERVIEW

INTERVIEW SELF-EVALUATION

	Strongly Agree	Agree	Neutral	Disagree	Strongly Disagree	Not Applicable
Coachability: I demonstrated an openness to feedback and a willingness to incorporate suggestions provided by colleagues and management.	☐	☐	☐	☐	☐	☐
Clinical Data Interpretation: I demonstrated the ability to interpret and discuss clinical data effectively.	☐	☐	☐	☐	☐	☐
Flexibility: I demonstrated flexibility and adaptability in responding to unexpected questions or situations.	☐	☐	☐	☐	☐	☐
Overall Confidence: I felt confident and poised throughout the interview.	☐	☐	☐	☐	☐	☐
Handling Challenging Questions: I effectively navigated and responded to challenging or unexpected questions during the interview.	☐	☐	☐	☐	☐	☐
Succinct Responses to Interview Questions: I responded succinctly to interview questions, providing clear and concise answers without unnecessary elaboration.	☐	☐	☐	☐	☐	☐
Competitor Knowledge: I demonstrated knowledge of the competitive landscape and effectively communicated distinctions between the company's products and its competitors.	☐	☐	☐	☐	☐	☐

www.themslbook.com

MSL JOB APPLICATION TRACKING & INTERVIEW SELF-EVALUATION JOURNAL

INTERVIEW SELF-EVALUATION

	Strongly Agree	Agree	Neutral	Disagree	Strongly Disagree	Not Applicable
Strategic Thinking: I demonstrated strategic thinking in discussing how the company's products fit into the broader healthcare landscape.	☐	☐	☐	☐	☐	☐
Digital Communication Skills: I effectively conveyed my proficiency in utilizing digital communication tools for scientific engagement.	☐	☐	☐	☐	☐	☐
Continual Learning: I highlighted my commitment to continual learning and staying updated on advancements in the therapeutic area.	☐	☐	☐	☐	☐	☐
Team Collaboration: I emphasized my ability to collaborate effectively with team members and cross-functional teams.	☐	☐	☐	☐	☐	☐
Enthusiasm for the Role: I effectively conveyed genuine enthusiasm for the role and the science of the product.	☐	☐	☐	☐	☐	☐
Asking Relevant Questions: I proactively asked relevant questions during the interview, demonstrating a genuine interest and understanding of the role.	☐	☐	☐	☐	☐	☐
STAR Method Application: When expected, I effectively utilized the STAR (Situation, Task, Action, Result) method when responding to behavioral questions.	☐	☐	☐	☐	☐	☐

MSL JOB APPLICATION TRACKING & INTERVIEW SELF-EVALUATION JOURNAL

2nd INTERVIEW

PRESENTATION SELF-EVALUATION*

	Strongly Agree	Agree	Neutral	Disagree	Strongly Disagree
Clarity of Message: I clearly and effectively communicated the key points of my presentation.	☐	☐	☐	☐	☐
Engagement with Audience: I maintained audience engagement by using effective visuals, body language, and vocal tone.	☐	☐	☐	☐	☐
Knowledge Demonstration: I demonstrated a comprehensive understanding of the subject matter and responded confidently to questions.	☐	☐	☐	☐	☐
Visual Aids Effectiveness: The visual aids (slides, charts, etc.) I utilized enhanced the overall impact of my presentation.	☐	☐	☐	☐	☐
Time Management: I effectively utilized the allotted time, ensuring all key points were covered within the specified timeframe.	☐	☐	☐	☐	☐
Adaptability to Audience: I adapted my presentation style to suit the needs and level of understanding of the audience.	☐	☐	☐	☐	☐
Overall Confidence: I felt confident and poised throughout the presentation.	☐	☐	☐	☐	☐
Communicating Scientific Information: I demonstrated strong presentation skills in conveying scientific information to a diverse audience.	☐	☐	☐	☐	☐

*Although most applicants will be expected to deliver a presentation once during the interview process (typically during the in-person interview), it's important to be prepared to present at any point throughout the process.

MSL JOB APPLICATION TRACKING & INTERVIEW SELF-EVALUATION JOURNAL

2nd INTERVIEW

THANK-YOU LETTER

Date Sent: _____/_____/_____

Individual's Name:

Email Address:

NOTES

_____
_____
_____
_____
_____
_____
_____
_____
_____
_____
_____

MSL JOB APPLICATION TRACKING & INTERVIEW SELF-EVALUATION JOURNAL

3rd INTERVIEW

INTERVIEW DETAILS

Position Applied For: Company:

INTERVIEW DATE, TIME, FORMAT

Scheduled Interview Date: _____/_____/_____   ☐ Phone Interview

Scheduled Interview Time: ____ : ____ ☐ AM ☐ PM   ☐ Virtual Interview

                                                    ☐ In-Person Interview

Interviewer Details

Names and Titles of Interviewer(s):

1. _____   4. _____

2. _____   5. _____

3. _____   6. _____

What I Did Well   ## What I Can Improve

MSL JOB APPLICATION TRACKING & INTERVIEW SELF-EVALUATION JOURNAL

3rd INTERVIEW

INTERVIEW QUESTIONS

Which questions were most challenging to answer?

1. _____
2. _____
3. _____
4. _____

Key questions you were asked:

1. _____
2. _____
3. _____
4. _____

Self-assessment of my responses:

1. _____
2. _____
3. _____
4. _____

INTERVIEW SELF-EVALUATION

3rd INTERVIEW

	Strongly Agree	Agree	Neutral	Disagree	Strongly Disagree	Not Applicable
Disease State / Therapeutic Area Expertise: I effectively communicated my expertise in the specific disease state and therapeutic area relevant to the role.	☐	☐	☐	☐	☐	☐
KOL Engagement: I effectively communicated my experience engaging Key Opinion Leaders (KOLs) and Health Care Providers (HCPs).	☐	☐	☐	☐	☐	☐
Product Knowledge: I demonstrated a deep understanding of the company's products and their clinical applications.	☐	☐	☐	☐	☐	☐
Clinical Trial Knowledge: I demonstrated a solid understanding of clinical trial methodologies and their relevance.	☐	☐	☐	☐	☐	☐
Regulatory/Compliance Knowledge: I highlighted knowledge of regulatory guidelines and compliance standards relevant to the role.	☐	☐	☐	☐	☐	☐
Relationship Building: I highlighted my experience in building and maintaining professional relationships both internally and externally.	☐	☐	☐	☐	☐	☐

INTERVIEW SELF-EVALUATION

3rd INTERVIEW

	Strongly Agree	Agree	Neutral	Disagree	Strongly Disagree	Not Applicable
Coachability: I demonstrated an openness to feedback and a willingness to incorporate suggestions provided by colleagues and management.	☐	☐	☐	☐	☐	☐
Clinical Data Interpretation: I demonstrated the ability to interpret and discuss clinical data effectively.	☐	☐	☐	☐	☐	☐
Flexibility: I demonstrated flexibility and adaptability in responding to unexpected questions or situations.	☐	☐	☐	☐	☐	☐
Overall Confidence: I felt confident and poised throughout the interview.	☐	☐	☐	☐	☐	☐
Handling Challenging Questions: I effectively navigated and responded to challenging or unexpected questions during the interview.	☐	☐	☐	☐	☐	☐
Succinct Responses to Interview Questions: I responded succinctly to interview questions, providing clear and concise answers without unnecessary elaboration.	☐	☐	☐	☐	☐	☐
Competitor Knowledge: I demonstrated knowledge of the competitive landscape and effectively communicated distinctions between the company's products and its competitors.	☐	☐	☐	☐	☐	☐

INTERVIEW SELF-EVALUATION

	Strongly Agree	Agree	Neutral	Disagree	Strongly Disagree	Not Applicable
Strategic Thinking: I demonstrated strategic thinking in discussing how the company's products fit into the broader healthcare landscape.	☐	☐	☐	☐	☐	☐
Digital Communication Skills: I effectively conveyed my proficiency in utilizing digital communication tools for scientific engagement.	☐	☐	☐	☐	☐	☐
Continual Learning: I highlighted my commitment to continual learning and staying updated on advancements in the therapeutic area.	☐	☐	☐	☐	☐	☐
Team Collaboration: I emphasized my ability to collaborate effectively with team members and cross-functional teams.	☐	☐	☐	☐	☐	☐
Enthusiasm for the Role: I effectively conveyed genuine enthusiasm for the role and the science of the product.	☐	☐	☐	☐	☐	☐
Asking Relevant Questions: I proactively asked relevant questions during the interview, demonstrating a genuine interest and understanding of the role.	☐	☐	☐	☐	☐	☐
STAR Method Application: When expected, I effectively utilized the STAR (Situation, Task, Action, Result) method when responding to behavioral questions.	☐	☐	☐	☐	☐	☐

MSL JOB APPLICATION TRACKING & INTERVIEW SELF-EVALUATION JOURNAL

3rd INTERVIEW

PRESENTATION SELF-EVALUATION*

	Strongly Agree	Agree	Neutral	Disagree	Strongly Disagree
Clarity of Message: I clearly and effectively communicated the key points of my presentation.	☐	☐	☐	☐	☐
Engagement with Audience: I maintained audience engagement by using effective visuals, body language, and vocal tone.	☐	☐	☐	☐	☐
Knowledge Demonstration: I demonstrated a comprehensive understanding of the subject matter and responded confidently to questions.	☐	☐	☐	☐	☐
Visual Aids Effectiveness: The visual aids (slides, charts, etc.) I utilized enhanced the overall impact of my presentation.	☐	☐	☐	☐	☐
Time Management: I effectively utilized the allotted time, ensuring all key points were covered within the specified timeframe.	☐	☐	☐	☐	☐
Adaptability to Audience: I adapted my presentation style to suit the needs and level of understanding of the audience.	☐	☐	☐	☐	☐
Overall Confidence: I felt confident and poised throughout the presentation.	☐	☐	☐	☐	☐
Communicating Scientific Information: I demonstrated strong presentation skills in conveying scientific information to a diverse audience.	☐	☐	☐	☐	☐

*Although most applicants will be expected to deliver a presentation once during the interview process (typically during the in-person interview), it's important to be prepared to present at any point throughout the process.

3rd INTERVIEW

THANK-YOU LETTER

Date Sent: _____/_____/_____

Individual's Name:

Email Address:

NOTES

_____
_____
_____
_____
_____
_____
_____
_____
_____
_____

MSL JOB APPLICATION TRACKING & INTERVIEW SELF-EVALUATION JOURNAL

4th INTERVIEW

INTERVIEW DETAILS

Position Applied For: _____   Company: _____

INTERVIEW DATE, TIME, FORMAT

Scheduled Interview Date: _____/_____/_____

Scheduled Interview Time: ____:____ ☐ AM ☐ PM

☐ Phone Interview
☐ Virtual Interview
☐ In-Person Interview

Interviewer Details

Names and Titles of Interviewer(s):

1. _____
2. _____
3. _____
4. _____
5. _____
6. _____

What I Did Well

_____
_____
_____
_____

What I Can Improve

_____
_____
_____
_____

MSL JOB APPLICATION TRACKING & INTERVIEW SELF-EVALUATION JOURNAL

4th INTERVIEW

INTERVIEW QUESTIONS

Which questions were most challenging to answer?

1. _____
2. _____
3. _____
4. _____

Key questions you were asked:

1. _____
2. _____
3. _____
4. _____

Self-assessment of my responses:

1. _____
2. _____
3. _____
4. _____

INTERVIEW SELF-EVALUATION

	Strongly Agree	Agree	Neutral	Disagree	Strongly Disagree	Not Applicable
Disease State / Therapeutic Area Expertise: I effectively communicated my expertise in the specific disease state and therapeutic area relevant to the role.	☐	☐	☐	☐	☐	☐
KOL Engagement: I effectively communicated my experience engaging Key Opinion Leaders (KOLs) and Health Care Providers (HCPs).	☐	☐	☐	☐	☐	☐
Product Knowledge: I demonstrated a deep understanding of the company's products and their clinical applications.	☐	☐	☐	☐	☐	☐
Clinical Trial Knowledge: I demonstrated a solid understanding of clinical trial methodologies and their relevance.	☐	☐	☐	☐	☐	☐
Regulatory/Compliance Knowledge: I highlighted knowledge of regulatory guidelines and compliance standards relevant to the role.	☐	☐	☐	☐	☐	☐
Relationship Building: I highlighted my experience in building and maintaining professional relationships both internally and externally.	☐	☐	☐	☐	☐	☐

INTERVIEW SELF-EVALUATION

4th INTERVIEW

	Strongly Agree	Agree	Neutral	Disagree	Strongly Disagree	Not Applicable
Coachability: I demonstrated an openness to feedback and a willingness to incorporate suggestions provided by colleagues and management.	☐	☐	☐	☐	☐	☐
Clinical Data Interpretation: I demonstrated the ability to interpret and discuss clinical data effectively.	☐	☐	☐	☐	☐	☐
Flexibility: I demonstrated flexibility and adaptability in responding to unexpected questions or situations.	☐	☐	☐	☐	☐	☐
Overall Confidence: I felt confident and poised throughout the interview.	☐	☐	☐	☐	☐	☐
Handling Challenging Questions: I effectively navigated and responded to challenging or unexpected questions during the interview.	☐	☐	☐	☐	☐	☐
Succinct Responses to Interview Questions: I responded succinctly to interview questions, providing clear and concise answers without unnecessary elaboration.	☐	☐	☐	☐	☐	☐
Competitor Knowledge: I demonstrated knowledge of the competitive landscape and effectively communicated distinctions between the company's products and its competitors.	☐	☐	☐	☐	☐	☐

INTERVIEW SELF-EVALUATION

4th INTERVIEW

	Strongly Agree	Agree	Neutral	Disagree	Strongly Disagree	Not Applicable
Strategic Thinking: I demonstrated strategic thinking in discussing how the company's products fit into the broader healthcare landscape.	☐	☐	☐	☐	☐	☐
Digital Communication Skills: I effectively conveyed my proficiency in utilizing digital communication tools for scientific engagement.	☐	☐	☐	☐	☐	☐
Continual Learning: I highlighted my commitment to continual learning and staying updated on advancements in the therapeutic area.	☐	☐	☐	☐	☐	☐
Team Collaboration: I emphasized my ability to collaborate effectively with team members and cross-functional teams.	☐	☐	☐	☐	☐	☐
Enthusiasm for the Role: I effectively conveyed genuine enthusiasm for the role and the science of the product.	☐	☐	☐	☐	☐	☐
Asking Relevant Questions: I proactively asked relevant questions during the interview, demonstrating a genuine interest and understanding of the role.	☐	☐	☐	☐	☐	☐
STAR Method Application: When expected, I effectively utilized the STAR (Situation, Task, Action, Result) method when responding to behavioral questions.	☐	☐	☐	☐	☐	☐

www.themslbook.com

MSL JOB APPLICATION TRACKING & INTERVIEW SELF-EVALUATION JOURNAL

4th INTERVIEW

PRESENTATION SELF-EVALUATION*

	Strongly Agree	Agree	Neutral	Disagree	Strongly Disagree
Clarity of Message: I clearly and effectively communicated the key points of my presentation.	☐	☐	☐	☐	☐
Engagement with Audience: I maintained audience engagement by using effective visuals, body language, and vocal tone.	☐	☐	☐	☐	☐
Knowledge Demonstration: I demonstrated a comprehensive understanding of the subject matter and responded confidently to questions.	☐	☐	☐	☐	☐
Visual Aids Effectiveness: The visual aids (slides, charts, etc.) I utilized enhanced the overall impact of my presentation.	☐	☐	☐	☐	☐
Time Management: I effectively utilized the allotted time, ensuring all key points were covered within the specified timeframe.	☐	☐	☐	☐	☐
Adaptability to Audience: I adapted my presentation style to suit the needs and level of understanding of the audience.	☐	☐	☐	☐	☐
Overall Confidence: I felt confident and poised throughout the presentation.	☐	☐	☐	☐	☐
Communicating Scientific Information: I demonstrated strong presentation skills in conveying scientific information to a diverse audience.	☐	☐	☐	☐	☐

*Although most applicants will be expected to deliver a presentation once during the interview process (typically during the in-person interview), it's important to be prepared to present at any point throughout the process.

MSL JOB APPLICATION TRACKING & INTERVIEW SELF-EVALUATION JOURNAL

4th INTERVIEW

THANK-YOU LETTER

Date Sent: _____/_____/_____

Individual's Name:

Email Address:

NOTES

_____
_____
_____
_____
_____
_____
_____
_____
_____
_____
_____

INTERVIEW TRACKING

MSL JOB APPLICATION TRACKING & INTERVIEW SELF-EVALUATION JOURNAL

1st INTERVIEW

INTERVIEW DETAILS

Position Applied For: Company:

INTERVIEW DATE, TIME, FORMAT

Scheduled Interview Date: _____/_____/_____

Scheduled Interview Time: _____ : _____ ☐ AM ☐ PM

☐ Phone Interview
☐ Virtual Interview
☐ In-Person Interview

Interviewer Details

Names and Titles of Interviewer(s):

1. _____
2. _____
3. _____
4. _____
5. _____
6. _____

What I Did Well

_____

_____

_____

_____

What I Can Improve

_____

_____

_____

_____

www.themslbook.com

MSL JOB APPLICATION TRACKING & INTERVIEW SELF-EVALUATION JOURNAL

1st INTERVIEW

INTERVIEW QUESTIONS

Which questions were most challenging to answer?

1. _____

2. _____

3. _____

4. _____

Key questions you were asked:

1. _____

2. _____

3. _____

4. _____

Self-assessment of my responses:

1. _____

2. _____

3. _____

4. _____

INTERVIEW SELF-EVALUATION

1st INTERVIEW

	Strongly Agree	Agree	Neutral	Disagree	Strongly Disagree	Not Applicable
Disease State / Therapeutic Area Expertise: I effectively communicated my expertise in the specific disease state and therapeutic area relevant to the role.	☐	☐	☐	☐	☐	☐
KOL Engagement: I effectively communicated my experience engaging Key Opinion Leaders (KOLs) and Health Care Providers (HCPs).	☐	☐	☐	☐	☐	☐
Product Knowledge: I demonstrated a deep understanding of the company's products and their clinical applications.	☐	☐	☐	☐	☐	☐
Clinical Trial Knowledge: I demonstrated a solid understanding of clinical trial methodologies and their relevance.	☐	☐	☐	☐	☐	☐
Regulatory/Compliance Knowledge: I highlighted knowledge of regulatory guidelines and compliance standards relevant to the role.	☐	☐	☐	☐	☐	☐
Relationship Building: I highlighted my experience in building and maintaining professional relationships both internally and externally.	☐	☐	☐	☐	☐	☐

INTERVIEW SELF-EVALUATION

1st INTERVIEW

	Strongly Agree	Agree	Neutral	Disagree	Strongly Disagree	Not Applicable
Coachability: I demonstrated an openness to feedback and a willingness to incorporate suggestions provided by colleagues and management.	☐	☐	☐	☐	☐	☐
Clinical Data Interpretation: I demonstrated the ability to interpret and discuss clinical data effectively.	☐	☐	☐	☐	☐	☐
Flexibility: I demonstrated flexibility and adaptability in responding to unexpected questions or situations.	☐	☐	☐	☐	☐	☐
Overall Confidence: I felt confident and poised throughout the interview.	☐	☐	☐	☐	☐	☐
Handling Challenging Questions: I effectively navigated and responded to challenging or unexpected questions during the interview.	☐	☐	☐	☐	☐	☐
Succinct Responses to Interview Questions: I responded succinctly to interview questions, providing clear and concise answers without unnecessary elaboration.	☐	☐	☐	☐	☐	☐
Competitor Knowledge: I demonstrated knowledge of the competitive landscape and effectively communicated distinctions between the company's products and its competitors.	☐	☐	☐	☐	☐	☐

MSL JOB APPLICATION TRACKING & INTERVIEW SELF-EVALUATION JOURNAL

1st INTERVIEW

INTERVIEW SELF-EVALUATION

	Strongly Agree	Agree	Neutral	Disagree	Strongly Disagree	Not Applicable
Strategic Thinking: I demonstrated strategic thinking in discussing how the company's products fit into the broader healthcare landscape.	☐	☐	☐	☐	☐	☐
Digital Communication Skills: I effectively conveyed my proficiency in utilizing digital communication tools for scientific engagement.	☐	☐	☐	☐	☐	☐
Continual Learning: I highlighted my commitment to continual learning and staying updated on advancements in the therapeutic area.	☐	☐	☐	☐	☐	☐
Team Collaboration: I emphasized my ability to collaborate effectively with team members and cross-functional teams.	☐	☐	☐	☐	☐	☐
Enthusiasm for the Role: I effectively conveyed genuine enthusiasm for the role and the science of the product.	☐	☐	☐	☐	☐	☐
Asking Relevant Questions: I proactively asked relevant questions during the interview, demonstrating a genuine interest and understanding of the role.	☐	☐	☐	☐	☐	☐
STAR Method Application: When expected, I effectively utilized the STAR (Situation, Task, Action, Result) method when responding to behavioral questions.	☐	☐	☐	☐	☐	☐

www.themslbook.com

PRESENTATION SELF-EVALUATION*

1st INTERVIEW

	Strongly Agree	Agree	Neutral	Disagree	Strongly Disagree
Clarity of Message: I clearly and effectively communicated the key points of my presentation.	☐	☐	☐	☐	☐
Engagement with Audience: I maintained audience engagement by using effective visuals, body language, and vocal tone.	☐	☐	☐	☐	☐
Knowledge Demonstration: I demonstrated a comprehensive understanding of the subject matter and responded confidently to questions.	☐	☐	☐	☐	☐
Visual Aids Effectiveness: The visual aids (slides, charts, etc.) I utilized enhanced the overall impact of my presentation.	☐	☐	☐	☐	☐
Time Management: I effectively utilized the allotted time, ensuring all key points were covered within the specified timeframe.	☐	☐	☐	☐	☐
Adaptability to Audience: I adapted my presentation style to suit the needs and level of understanding of the audience.	☐	☐	☐	☐	☐
Overall Confidence: I felt confident and poised throughout the presentation.	☐	☐	☐	☐	☐
Communicating Scientific Information: I demonstrated strong presentation skills in conveying scientific information to a diverse audience.	☐	☐	☐	☐	☐

*Although most applicants will be expected to deliver a presentation once during the interview process (typically during the in-person interview), it's important to be prepared to present at any point throughout the process.

MSL JOB APPLICATION TRACKING & INTERVIEW SELF-EVALUATION JOURNAL

1st INTERVIEW

THANK-YOU LETTER

Date Sent: _____/_____/_____

Individual's Name:

Email Address:

NOTES

_____
_____
_____
_____
_____
_____
_____
_____
_____
_____
_____

MSL JOB APPLICATION TRACKING & INTERVIEW SELF-EVALUATION JOURNAL

2nd INTERVIEW

INTERVIEW DETAILS

Position Applied For: _____   Company: _____

INTERVIEW DATE, TIME, FORMAT

Scheduled Interview Date: _____ / _____ / _____

Scheduled Interview Time: _____ : _____ ☐ AM ☐ PM

☐ Phone Interview
☐ Virtual Interview
☐ In-Person Interview

Interviewer Details

Names and Titles of Interviewer(s):

1. _____
2. _____
3. _____
4. _____
5. _____
6. _____

What I Did Well

_____
_____
_____
_____
_____

What I Can Improve

_____
_____
_____
_____
_____

MSL JOB APPLICATION TRACKING & INTERVIEW SELF-EVALUATION JOURNAL

2nd INTERVIEW

INTERVIEW QUESTIONS

Which questions were most challenging to answer?

1. _____

2. _____

3. _____

4. _____

Key questions you were asked:

1. _____

2. _____

3. _____

4. _____

Self-assessment of my responses:

1. _____

2. _____

3. _____

4. _____

INTERVIEW SELF-EVALUATION

2nd INTERVIEW

	Strongly Agree	Agree	Neutral	Disagree	Strongly Disagree	Not Applicable
Disease State / Therapeutic Area Expertise: I effectively communicated my expertise in the specific disease state and therapeutic area relevant to the role.	☐	☐	☐	☐	☐	☐
KOL Engagement: I effectively communicated my experience engaging Key Opinion Leaders (KOLs) and Health Care Providers (HCPs).	☐	☐	☐	☐	☐	☐
Product Knowledge: I demonstrated a deep understanding of the company's products and their clinical applications.	☐	☐	☐	☐	☐	☐
Clinical Trial Knowledge: I demonstrated a solid understanding of clinical trial methodologies and their relevance.	☐	☐	☐	☐	☐	☐
Regulatory/Compliance Knowledge: I highlighted knowledge of regulatory guidelines and compliance standards relevant to the role.	☐	☐	☐	☐	☐	☐
Relationship Building: I highlighted my experience in building and maintaining professional relationships both internally and externally.	☐	☐	☐	☐	☐	☐

INTERVIEW SELF-EVALUATION

2nd INTERVIEW

	Strongly Agree	Agree	Neutral	Disagree	Strongly Disagree	Not Applicable
Coachability: I demonstrated an openness to feedback and a willingness to incorporate suggestions provided by colleagues and management.	☐	☐	☐	☐	☐	☐
Clinical Data Interpretation: I demonstrated the ability to interpret and discuss clinical data effectively.	☐	☐	☐	☐	☐	☐
Flexibility: I demonstrated flexibility and adaptability in responding to unexpected questions or situations.	☐	☐	☐	☐	☐	☐
Overall Confidence: I felt confident and poised throughout the interview.	☐	☐	☐	☐	☐	☐
Handling Challenging Questions: I effectively navigated and responded to challenging or unexpected questions during the interview.	☐	☐	☐	☐	☐	☐
Succinct Responses to Interview Questions: I responded succinctly to interview questions, providing clear and concise answers without unnecessary elaboration.	☐	☐	☐	☐	☐	☐
Competitor Knowledge: I demonstrated knowledge of the competitive landscape and effectively communicated distinctions between the company's products and its competitors.	☐	☐	☐	☐	☐	☐

INTERVIEW SELF-EVALUATION

2nd INTERVIEW

	Strongly Agree	Agree	Neutral	Disagree	Strongly Disagree	Not Applicable
Strategic Thinking: I demonstrated strategic thinking in discussing how the company's products fit into the broader healthcare landscape.	☐	☐	☐	☐	☐	☐
Digital Communication Skills: I effectively conveyed my proficiency in utilizing digital communication tools for scientific engagement.	☐	☐	☐	☐	☐	☐
Continual Learning: I highlighted my commitment to continual learning and staying updated on advancements in the therapeutic area.	☐	☐	☐	☐	☐	☐
Team Collaboration: I emphasized my ability to collaborate effectively with team members and cross-functional teams.	☐	☐	☐	☐	☐	☐
Enthusiasm for the Role: I effectively conveyed genuine enthusiasm for the role and the science of the product.	☐	☐	☐	☐	☐	☐
Asking Relevant Questions: I proactively asked relevant questions during the interview, demonstrating a genuine interest and understanding of the role.	☐	☐	☐	☐	☐	☐
STAR Method Application: When expected, I effectively utilized the STAR (Situation, Task, Action, Result) method when responding to behavioral questions.	☐	☐	☐	☐	☐	☐

MSL JOB APPLICATION TRACKING & INTERVIEW SELF-EVALUATION JOURNAL

2nd INTERVIEW

PRESENTATION SELF-EVALUATION*

	Strongly Agree	Agree	Neutral	Disagree	Strongly Disagree
Clarity of Message: I clearly and effectively communicated the key points of my presentation.	☐	☐	☐	☐	☐
Engagement with Audience: I maintained audience engagement by using effective visuals, body language, and vocal tone.	☐	☐	☐	☐	☐
Knowledge Demonstration: I demonstrated a comprehensive understanding of the subject matter and responded confidently to questions.	☐	☐	☐	☐	☐
Visual Aids Effectiveness: The visual aids (slides, charts, etc.) I utilized enhanced the overall impact of my presentation.	☐	☐	☐	☐	☐
Time Management: I effectively utilized the allotted time, ensuring all key points were covered within the specified timeframe.	☐	☐	☐	☐	☐
Adaptability to Audience: I adapted my presentation style to suit the needs and level of understanding of the audience.	☐	☐	☐	☐	☐
Overall Confidence: I felt confident and poised throughout the presentation.	☐	☐	☐	☐	☐
Communicating Scientific Information: I demonstrated strong presentation skills in conveying scientific information to a diverse audience.	☐	☐	☐	☐	☐

*Although most applicants will be expected to deliver a presentation once during the interview process (typically during the in-person interview), it's important to be prepared to present at any point throughout the process.

www.themslbook.com

MSL JOB APPLICATION TRACKING & INTERVIEW SELF-EVALUATION JOURNAL

2nd INTERVIEW

THANK-YOU LETTER

Date Sent: _____/_____/_____

Individual's Name:

Email Address:

NOTES

_____

_____

_____

_____

_____

_____

_____

_____

_____

MSL JOB APPLICATION TRACKING & INTERVIEW SELF-EVALUATION JOURNAL

3rd INTERVIEW

INTERVIEW DETAILS

Position Applied For: Company:

INTERVIEW DATE, TIME, FORMAT

Scheduled Interview Date: _____/_____/_____

Scheduled Interview Time: _____:_____ ☐ AM ☐ PM

☐ Phone Interview
☐ Virtual Interview
☐ In-Person Interview

Interviewer Details

Names and Titles of Interviewer(s):

1. _____
2. _____
3. _____
4. _____
5. _____
6. _____

What I Did Well

_____

_____

_____

_____

What I Can Improve

_____

_____

_____

_____

MSL JOB APPLICATION TRACKING & INTERVIEW SELF-EVALUATION JOURNAL

3rd INTERVIEW

INTERVIEW QUESTIONS

Which questions were most challenging to answer?

1. _____
2. _____
3. _____
4. _____

Key questions you were asked:

1. _____
2. _____
3. _____
4. _____

Self-assessment of my responses:

1. _____
2. _____
3. _____
4. _____

MSL JOB APPLICATION TRACKING & INTERVIEW SELF-EVALUATION JOURNAL

INTERVIEW SELF-EVALUATION

	Strongly Agree	Agree	Neutral	Disagree	Strongly Disagree	Not Applicable
Disease State / Therapeutic Area Expertise: I effectively communicated my expertise in the specific disease state and therapeutic area relevant to the role.	☐	☐	☐	☐	☐	☐
KOL Engagement: I effectively communicated my experience engaging Key Opinion Leaders (KOLs) and Health Care Providers (HCPs).	☐	☐	☐	☐	☐	☐
Product Knowledge: I demonstrated a deep understanding of the company's products and their clinical applications.	☐	☐	☐	☐	☐	☐
Clinical Trial Knowledge: I demonstrated a solid understanding of clinical trial methodologies and their relevance.	☐	☐	☐	☐	☐	☐
Regulatory/Compliance Knowledge: I highlighted knowledge of regulatory guidelines and compliance standards relevant to the role.	☐	☐	☐	☐	☐	☐
Relationship Building: I highlighted my experience in building and maintaining professional relationships both internally and externally.	☐	☐	☐	☐	☐	☐

INTERVIEW SELF-EVALUATION

3rd INTERVIEW

	Strongly Agree	Agree	Neutral	Disagree	Strongly Disagree	Not Applicable
Coachability: I demonstrated an openness to feedback and a willingness to incorporate suggestions provided by colleagues and management.	☐	☐	☐	☐	☐	☐
Clinical Data Interpretation: I demonstrated the ability to interpret and discuss clinical data effectively.	☐	☐	☐	☐	☐	☐
Flexibility: I demonstrated flexibility and adaptability in responding to unexpected questions or situations.	☐	☐	☐	☐	☐	☐
Overall Confidence: I felt confident and poised throughout the interview.	☐	☐	☐	☐	☐	☐
Handling Challenging Questions: I effectively navigated and responded to challenging or unexpected questions during the interview.	☐	☐	☐	☐	☐	☐
Succinct Responses to Interview Questions: I responded succinctly to interview questions, providing clear and concise answers without unnecessary elaboration.	☐	☐	☐	☐	☐	☐
Competitor Knowledge: I demonstrated knowledge of the competitive landscape and effectively communicated distinctions between the company's products and its competitors.	☐	☐	☐	☐	☐	☐

MSL JOB APPLICATION TRACKING & INTERVIEW SELF-EVALUATION JOURNAL

INTERVIEW SELF-EVALUATION

3rd INTERVIEW

	Strongly Agree	Agree	Neutral	Disagree	Strongly Disagree	Not Applicable
Strategic Thinking: I demonstrated strategic thinking in discussing how the company's products fit into the broader healthcare landscape.	☐	☐	☐	☐	☐	☐
Digital Communication Skills: I effectively conveyed my proficiency in utilizing digital communication tools for scientific engagement.	☐	☐	☐	☐	☐	☐
Continual Learning: I highlighted my commitment to continual learning and staying updated on advancements in the therapeutic area.	☐	☐	☐	☐	☐	☐
Team Collaboration: I emphasized my ability to collaborate effectively with team members and cross-functional teams.	☐	☐	☐	☐	☐	☐
Enthusiasm for the Role: I effectively conveyed genuine enthusiasm for the role and the science of the product.	☐	☐	☐	☐	☐	☐
Asking Relevant Questions: I proactively asked relevant questions during the interview, demonstrating a genuine interest and understanding of the role.	☐	☐	☐	☐	☐	☐
STAR Method Application: When expected, I effectively utilized the STAR (Situation, Task, Action, Result) method when responding to behavioral questions.	☐	☐	☐	☐	☐	☐

www.themslbook.com

MSL JOB APPLICATION TRACKING & INTERVIEW SELF-EVALUATION JOURNAL

PRESENTATION SELF-EVALUATION*

3rd INTERVIEW

	Strongly Agree	Agree	Neutral	Disagree	Strongly Disagree
Clarity of Message: I clearly and effectively communicated the key points of my presentation.	☐	☐	☐	☐	☐
Engagement with Audience: I maintained audience engagement by using effective visuals, body language, and vocal tone.	☐	☐	☐	☐	☐
Knowledge Demonstration: I demonstrated a comprehensive understanding of the subject matter and responded confidently to questions.	☐	☐	☐	☐	☐
Visual Aids Effectiveness: The visual aids (slides, charts, etc.) I utilized enhanced the overall impact of my presentation.	☐	☐	☐	☐	☐
Time Management: I effectively utilized the allotted time, ensuring all key points were covered within the specified timeframe.	☐	☐	☐	☐	☐
Adaptability to Audience: I adapted my presentation style to suit the needs and level of understanding of the audience.	☐	☐	☐	☐	☐
Overall Confidence: I felt confident and poised throughout the presentation.	☐	☐	☐	☐	☐
Communicating Scientific Information: I demonstrated strong presentation skills in conveying scientific information to a diverse audience.	☐	☐	☐	☐	☐

*Although most applicants will be expected to deliver a presentation once during the interview process (typically during the in-person interview), it's important to be prepared to present at any point throughout the process.

MSL JOB APPLICATION TRACKING & INTERVIEW SELF-EVALUATION JOURNAL

3rd INTERVIEW

THANK-YOU LETTER

Date Sent: _____/_____/_____

Individual's Name:

Email Address:

NOTES

_____

_____

_____

_____

_____

_____

_____

_____

_____

_____

_____

_____

MSL JOB APPLICATION TRACKING & INTERVIEW SELF-EVALUATION JOURNAL

4th INTERVIEW

INTERVIEW DETAILS

Position Applied For: Company:

INTERVIEW DATE, TIME, FORMAT

Scheduled Interview Date: _____ / _____ / _____

Scheduled Interview Time: ____ : ____ ☐ AM ☐ PM

☐ Phone Interview
☐ Virtual Interview
☐ In-Person Interview

Interviewer Details

Names and Titles of Interviewer(s):

1. _____   4. _____

2. _____   5. _____

3. _____   6. _____

What I Did Well   ## What I Can Improve

MSL JOB APPLICATION TRACKING & INTERVIEW SELF-EVALUATION JOURNAL

4th INTERVIEW

INTERVIEW QUESTIONS

Which questions were most challenging to answer?

1. _____
2. _____
3. _____
4. _____

Key questions you were asked:

1. _____
2. _____
3. _____
4. _____

Self-assessment of my responses:

1. _____
2. _____
3. _____
4. _____

www.themslbook.com   97

INTERVIEW SELF-EVALUATION

4th INTERVIEW

	Strongly Agree	Agree	Neutral	Disagree	Strongly Disagree	Not Applicable
Disease State / Therapeutic Area Expertise: I effectively communicated my expertise in the specific disease state and therapeutic area relevant to the role.	☐	☐	☐	☐	☐	☐
KOL Engagement: I effectively communicated my experience engaging Key Opinion Leaders (KOLs) and Health Care Providers (HCPs).	☐	☐	☐	☐	☐	☐
Product Knowledge: I demonstrated a deep understanding of the company's products and their clinical applications.	☐	☐	☐	☐	☐	☐
Clinical Trial Knowledge: I demonstrated a solid understanding of clinical trial methodologies and their relevance.	☐	☐	☐	☐	☐	☐
Regulatory/Compliance Knowledge: I highlighted knowledge of regulatory guidelines and compliance standards relevant to the role.	☐	☐	☐	☐	☐	☐
Relationship Building: I highlighted my experience in building and maintaining professional relationships both internally and externally.	☐	☐	☐	☐	☐	☐

MSL JOB APPLICATION TRACKING & INTERVIEW SELF-EVALUATION JOURNAL

INTERVIEW SELF-EVALUATION

4th INTERVIEW

	Strongly Agree	Agree	Neutral	Disagree	Strongly Disagree	Not Applicable
Coachability: I demonstrated an openness to feedback and a willingness to incorporate suggestions provided by colleagues and management.	☐	☐	☐	☐	☐	☐
Clinical Data Interpretation: I demonstrated the ability to interpret and discuss clinical data effectively.	☐	☐	☐	☐	☐	☐
Flexibility: I demonstrated flexibility and adaptability in responding to unexpected questions or situations.	☐	☐	☐	☐	☐	☐
Overall Confidence: I felt confident and poised throughout the interview.	☐	☐	☐	☐	☐	☐
Handling Challenging Questions: I effectively navigated and responded to challenging or unexpected questions during the interview.	☐	☐	☐	☐	☐	☐
Succinct Responses to Interview Questions: I responded succinctly to interview questions, providing clear and concise answers without unnecessary elaboration.	☐	☐	☐	☐	☐	☐
Competitor Knowledge: I demonstrated knowledge of the competitive landscape and effectively communicated distinctions between the company's products and its competitors.	☐	☐	☐	☐	☐	☐

www.themslbook.com

MSL JOB APPLICATION TRACKING & INTERVIEW SELF-EVALUATION JOURNAL

INTERVIEW SELF-EVALUATION

4th INTERVIEW

	Strongly Agree	Agree	Neutral	Disagree	Strongly Disagree	Not Applicable
Strategic Thinking: I demonstrated strategic thinking in discussing how the company's products fit into the broader healthcare landscape.	☐	☐	☐	☐	☐	☐
Digital Communication Skills: I effectively conveyed my proficiency in utilizing digital communication tools for scientific engagement.	☐	☐	☐	☐	☐	☐
Continual Learning: I highlighted my commitment to continual learning and staying updated on advancements in the therapeutic area.	☐	☐	☐	☐	☐	☐
Team Collaboration: I emphasized my ability to collaborate effectively with team members and cross-functional teams.	☐	☐	☐	☐	☐	☐
Enthusiasm for the Role: I effectively conveyed genuine enthusiasm for the role and the science of the product.	☐	☐	☐	☐	☐	☐
Asking Relevant Questions: I proactively asked relevant questions during the interview, demonstrating a genuine interest and understanding of the role.	☐	☐	☐	☐	☐	☐
STAR Method Application: When expected, I effectively utilized the STAR (Situation, Task, Action, Result) method when responding to behavioral questions.	☐	☐	☐	☐	☐	☐

www.themslbook.com

MSL JOB APPLICATION TRACKING & INTERVIEW SELF-EVALUATION JOURNAL

4th INTERVIEW

PRESENTATION SELF-EVALUATION*

	Strongly Agree	Agree	Neutral	Disagree	Strongly Disagree
Clarity of Message: I clearly and effectively communicated the key points of my presentation.	☐	☐	☐	☐	☐
Engagement with Audience: I maintained audience engagement by using effective visuals, body language, and vocal tone.	☐	☐	☐	☐	☐
Knowledge Demonstration: I demonstrated a comprehensive understanding of the subject matter and responded confidently to questions.	☐	☐	☐	☐	☐
Visual Aids Effectiveness: The visual aids (slides, charts, etc.) I utilized enhanced the overall impact of my presentation.	☐	☐	☐	☐	☐
Time Management: I effectively utilized the allotted time, ensuring all key points were covered within the specified timeframe.	☐	☐	☐	☐	☐
Adaptability to Audience: I adapted my presentation style to suit the needs and level of understanding of the audience.	☐	☐	☐	☐	☐
Overall Confidence: I felt confident and poised throughout the presentation.	☐	☐	☐	☐	☐
Communicating Scientific Information: I demonstrated strong presentation skills in conveying scientific information to a diverse audience.	☐	☐	☐	☐	☐

*Although most applicants will be expected to deliver a presentation once during the interview process (typically during the in-person interview), it's important to be prepared to present at any point throughout the process.

www.themslbook.com

MSL JOB APPLICATION TRACKING & INTERVIEW SELF-EVALUATION JOURNAL

4th INTERVIEW

THANK-YOU LETTER

Date Sent: _____/_____/_____

Individual's Name:

Email Address:

NOTES

_____
_____
_____
_____
_____
_____
_____
_____
_____
_____
_____

INTERVIEW TRACKING

MSL JOB APPLICATION TRACKING & INTERVIEW SELF-EVALUATION JOURNAL

1st INTERVIEW

INTERVIEW DETAILS

Position Applied For: _____   Company: _____

INTERVIEW DATE, TIME, FORMAT

Scheduled Interview Date: _____/_____/_____

Scheduled Interview Time: _____:_____ ☐ AM ☐ PM

☐ Phone Interview
☐ Virtual Interview
☐ In-Person Interview

Interviewer Details

Names and Titles of Interviewer(s):

1. _____   4. _____
2. _____   5. _____
3. _____   6. _____

What I Did Well

_____
_____
_____
_____
_____

What I Can Improve

_____
_____
_____
_____
_____

MSL JOB APPLICATION TRACKING & INTERVIEW SELF-EVALUATION JOURNAL

1st INTERVIEW

INTERVIEW QUESTIONS

Which questions were most challenging to answer?

1. _____
2. _____
3. _____
4. _____

Key questions you were asked:

1. _____
2. _____
3. _____
4. _____

Self-assessment of my responses:

1. _____
2. _____
3. _____
4. _____

1st INTERVIEW

INTERVIEW SELF-EVALUATION

	Strongly Agree	Agree	Neutral	Disagree	Strongly Disagree	Not Applicable
Disease State / Therapeutic Area Expertise: I effectively communicated my expertise in the specific disease state and therapeutic area relevant to the role.	☐	☐	☐	☐	☐	☐
KOL Engagement: I effectively communicated my experience engaging Key Opinion Leaders (KOLs) and Health Care Providers (HCPs).	☐	☐	☐	☐	☐	☐
Product Knowledge: I demonstrated a deep understanding of the company's products and their clinical applications.	☐	☐	☐	☐	☐	☐
Clinical Trial Knowledge: I demonstrated a solid understanding of clinical trial methodologies and their relevance.	☐	☐	☐	☐	☐	☐
Regulatory/Compliance Knowledge: I highlighted knowledge of regulatory guidelines and compliance standards relevant to the role.	☐	☐	☐	☐	☐	☐
Relationship Building: I highlighted my experience in building and maintaining professional relationships both internally and externally.	☐	☐	☐	☐	☐	☐

MSL JOB APPLICATION TRACKING & INTERVIEW SELF-EVALUATION JOURNAL

1st INTERVIEW

INTERVIEW SELF-EVALUATION

	Strongly Agree	Agree	Neutral	Disagree	Strongly Disagree	Not Applicable
Coachability: I demonstrated an openness to feedback and a willingness to incorporate suggestions provided by colleagues and management.	☐	☐	☐	☐	☐	☐
Clinical Data Interpretation: I demonstrated the ability to interpret and discuss clinical data effectively.	☐	☐	☐	☐	☐	☐
Flexibility: I demonstrated flexibility and adaptability in responding to unexpected questions or situations.	☐	☐	☐	☐	☐	☐
Overall Confidence: I felt confident and poised throughout the interview.	☐	☐	☐	☐	☐	☐
Handling Challenging Questions: I effectively navigated and responded to challenging or unexpected questions during the interview.	☐	☐	☐	☐	☐	☐
Succinct Responses to Interview Questions: I responded succinctly to interview questions, providing clear and concise answers without unnecessary elaboration.	☐	☐	☐	☐	☐	☐
Competitor Knowledge: I demonstrated knowledge of the competitive landscape and effectively communicated distinctions between the company's products and its competitors.	☐	☐	☐	☐	☐	☐

INTERVIEW SELF-EVALUATION

1st INTERVIEW

	Strongly Agree	Agree	Neutral	Disagree	Strongly Disagree	Not Applicable
Strategic Thinking: I demonstrated strategic thinking in discussing how the company's products fit into the broader healthcare landscape.	☐	☐	☐	☐	☐	☐
Digital Communication Skills: I effectively conveyed my proficiency in utilizing digital communication tools for scientific engagement.	☐	☐	☐	☐	☐	☐
Continual Learning: I highlighted my commitment to continual learning and staying updated on advancements in the therapeutic area.	☐	☐	☐	☐	☐	☐
Team Collaboration: I emphasized my ability to collaborate effectively with team members and cross-functional teams.	☐	☐	☐	☐	☐	☐
Enthusiasm for the Role: I effectively conveyed genuine enthusiasm for the role and the science of the product.	☐	☐	☐	☐	☐	☐
Asking Relevant Questions: I proactively asked relevant questions during the interview, demonstrating a genuine interest and understanding of the role.	☐	☐	☐	☐	☐	☐
STAR Method Application: When expected, I effectively utilized the STAR (Situation, Task, Action, Result) method when responding to behavioral questions.	☐	☐	☐	☐	☐	☐

MSL JOB APPLICATION TRACKING & INTERVIEW SELF-EVALUATION JOURNAL

1st INTERVIEW

PRESENTATION SELF-EVALUATION*

	Strongly Agree	Agree	Neutral	Disagree	Strongly Disagree
Clarity of Message: I clearly and effectively communicated the key points of my presentation.	☐	☐	☐	☐	☐
Engagement with Audience: I maintained audience engagement by using effective visuals, body language, and vocal tone.	☐	☐	☐	☐	☐
Knowledge Demonstration: I demonstrated a comprehensive understanding of the subject matter and responded confidently to questions.	☐	☐	☐	☐	☐
Visual Aids Effectiveness: The visual aids (slides, charts, etc.) I utilized enhanced the overall impact of my presentation.	☐	☐	☐	☐	☐
Time Management: I effectively utilized the allotted time, ensuring all key points were covered within the specified timeframe.	☐	☐	☐	☐	☐
Adaptability to Audience: I adapted my presentation style to suit the needs and level of understanding of the audience.	☐	☐	☐	☐	☐
Overall Confidence: I felt confident and poised throughout the presentation.	☐	☐	☐	☐	☐
Communicating Scientific Information: I demonstrated strong presentation skills in conveying scientific information to a diverse audience.	☐	☐	☐	☐	☐

*Although most applicants will be expected to deliver a presentation once during the interview process (typically during the in-person interview), it's important to be prepared to present at any point throughout the process.

MSL JOB APPLICATION TRACKING & INTERVIEW SELF-EVALUATION JOURNAL

1st INTERVIEW

THANK-YOU LETTER

Date Sent: _____ / _____ / _____

Individual's Name:

Email Address:

NOTES

_____
_____
_____
_____
_____
_____
_____
_____
_____
_____

MSL JOB APPLICATION TRACKING & INTERVIEW SELF-EVALUATION JOURNAL

2nd INTERVIEW

INTERVIEW DETAILS

Position Applied For: _____   Company: _____

INTERVIEW DATE, TIME, FORMAT

Scheduled Interview Date: _____/_____/_____

Scheduled Interview Time: ____:____ ☐ AM ☐ PM

☐ Phone Interview
☐ Virtual Interview
☐ In-Person Interview

Interviewer Details

Names and Titles of Interviewer(s):

1. _____   4. _____
2. _____   5. _____
3. _____   6. _____

What I Did Well

_____
_____
_____
_____
_____

What I Can Improve

_____
_____
_____
_____
_____

MSL JOB APPLICATION TRACKING & INTERVIEW SELF-EVALUATION JOURNAL

2nd INTERVIEW

INTERVIEW QUESTIONS

Which questions were most challenging to answer?

1. _____

2. _____

3. _____

4. _____

Key questions you were asked:

1. _____

2. _____

3. _____

4. _____

Self-assessment of my responses:

1. _____

2. _____

3. _____

4. _____

INTERVIEW SELF-EVALUATION

2nd INTERVIEW

	Strongly Agree	Agree	Neutral	Disagree	Strongly Disagree	Not Applicable
Disease State / Therapeutic Area Expertise: I effectively communicated my expertise in the specific disease state and therapeutic area relevant to the role.	☐	☐	☐	☐	☐	☐
KOL Engagement: I effectively communicated my experience engaging Key Opinion Leaders (KOLs) and Health Care Providers (HCPs).	☐	☐	☐	☐	☐	☐
Product Knowledge: I demonstrated a deep understanding of the company's products and their clinical applications.	☐	☐	☐	☐	☐	☐
Clinical Trial Knowledge: I demonstrated a solid understanding of clinical trial methodologies and their relevance.	☐	☐	☐	☐	☐	☐
Regulatory/Compliance Knowledge: I highlighted knowledge of regulatory guidelines and compliance standards relevant to the role.	☐	☐	☐	☐	☐	☐
Relationship Building: I highlighted my experience in building and maintaining professional relationships both internally and externally.	☐	☐	☐	☐	☐	☐

INTERVIEW SELF-EVALUATION

2nd INTERVIEW

	Strongly Agree	Agree	Neutral	Disagree	Strongly Disagree	Not Applicable
Coachability: I demonstrated an openness to feedback and a willingness to incorporate suggestions provided by colleagues and management.	☐	☐	☐	☐	☐	☐
Clinical Data Interpretation: I demonstrated the ability to interpret and discuss clinical data effectively.	☐	☐	☐	☐	☐	☐
Flexibility: I demonstrated flexibility and adaptability in responding to unexpected questions or situations.	☐	☐	☐	☐	☐	☐
Overall Confidence: I felt confident and poised throughout the interview.	☐	☐	☐	☐	☐	☐
Handling Challenging Questions: I effectively navigated and responded to challenging or unexpected questions during the interview.	☐	☐	☐	☐	☐	☐
Succinct Responses to Interview Questions: I responded succinctly to interview questions, providing clear and concise answers without unnecessary elaboration.	☐	☐	☐	☐	☐	☐
Competitor Knowledge: I demonstrated knowledge of the competitive landscape and effectively communicated distinctions between the company's products and its competitors.	☐	☐	☐	☐	☐	☐

INTERVIEW SELF-EVALUATION

2nd INTERVIEW

	Strongly Agree	Agree	Neutral	Disagree	Strongly Disagree	Not Applicable
Strategic Thinking: I demonstrated strategic thinking in discussing how the company's products fit into the broader healthcare landscape.	☐	☐	☐	☐	☐	☐
Digital Communication Skills: I effectively conveyed my proficiency in utilizing digital communication tools for scientific engagement.	☐	☐	☐	☐	☐	☐
Continual Learning: I highlighted my commitment to continual learning and staying updated on advancements in the therapeutic area.	☐	☐	☐	☐	☐	☐
Team Collaboration: I emphasized my ability to collaborate effectively with team members and cross-functional teams.	☐	☐	☐	☐	☐	☐
Enthusiasm for the Role: I effectively conveyed genuine enthusiasm for the role and the science of the product.	☐	☐	☐	☐	☐	☐
Asking Relevant Questions: I proactively asked relevant questions during the interview, demonstrating a genuine interest and understanding of the role.	☐	☐	☐	☐	☐	☐
STAR Method Application: When expected, I effectively utilized the STAR (Situation, Task, Action, Result) method when responding to behavioral questions.	☐	☐	☐	☐	☐	☐

MSL JOB APPLICATION TRACKING & INTERVIEW SELF-EVALUATION JOURNAL

2nd INTERVIEW

PRESENTATION SELF-EVALUATION*

	Strongly Agree	Agree	Neutral	Disagree	Strongly Disagree
Clarity of Message: I clearly and effectively communicated the key points of my presentation.	☐	☐	☐	☐	☐
Engagement with Audience: I maintained audience engagement by using effective visuals, body language, and vocal tone.	☐	☐	☐	☐	☐
Knowledge Demonstration: I demonstrated a comprehensive understanding of the subject matter and responded confidently to questions.	☐	☐	☐	☐	☐
Visual Aids Effectiveness: The visual aids (slides, charts, etc.) I utilized enhanced the overall impact of my presentation.	☐	☐	☐	☐	☐
Time Management: I effectively utilized the allotted time, ensuring all key points were covered within the specified timeframe.	☐	☐	☐	☐	☐
Adaptability to Audience: I adapted my presentation style to suit the needs and level of understanding of the audience.	☐	☐	☐	☐	☐
Overall Confidence: I felt confident and poised throughout the presentation.	☐	☐	☐	☐	☐
Communicating Scientific Information: I demonstrated strong presentation skills in conveying scientific information to a diverse audience.	☐	☐	☐	☐	☐

*Although most applicants will be expected to deliver a presentation once during the interview process (typically during the in-person interview), it's important to be prepared to present at any point throughout the process.

MSL JOB APPLICATION TRACKING & INTERVIEW SELF-EVALUATION JOURNAL

2nd INTERVIEW

THANK-YOU LETTER

Date Sent: _____/_____/_____

Individual's Name:

Email Address:

NOTES

_____
_____
_____
_____
_____
_____
_____
_____
_____
_____
_____

MSL JOB APPLICATION TRACKING & INTERVIEW SELF-EVALUATION JOURNAL

3rd INTERVIEW

INTERVIEW DETAILS

Position Applied For: _____ Company: _____

INTERVIEW DATE, TIME, FORMAT

Scheduled Interview Date: _____/_____/_____

Scheduled Interview Time: ____:____ ☐ AM ☐ PM

☐ Phone Interview
☐ Virtual Interview
☐ In-Person Interview

Interviewer Details

Names and Titles of Interviewer(s):

1. _____
2. _____
3. _____
4. _____
5. _____
6. _____

What I Did Well

_____
_____
_____
_____

What I Can Improve

_____
_____
_____
_____

3rd INTERVIEW

MSL JOB APPLICATION TRACKING & INTERVIEW SELF-EVALUATION JOURNAL

INTERVIEW QUESTIONS

Which questions were most challenging to answer?

1. _____
2. _____
3. _____
4. _____

Key questions you were asked:

1. _____
2. _____
3. _____
4. _____

Self-assessment of my responses:

1. _____
2. _____
3. _____
4. _____

MSL JOB APPLICATION TRACKING & INTERVIEW SELF-EVALUATION JOURNAL

3rd INTERVIEW

INTERVIEW SELF-EVALUATION

	Strongly Agree	Agree	Neutral	Disagree	Strongly Disagree	Not Applicable
Disease State / Therapeutic Area Expertise: I effectively communicated my expertise in the specific disease state and therapeutic area relevant to the role.	☐	☐	☐	☐	☐	☐
KOL Engagement: I effectively communicated my experience engaging Key Opinion Leaders (KOLs) and Health Care Providers (HCPs).	☐	☐	☐	☐	☐	☐
Product Knowledge: I demonstrated a deep understanding of the company's products and their clinical applications.	☐	☐	☐	☐	☐	☐
Clinical Trial Knowledge: I demonstrated a solid understanding of clinical trial methodologies and their relevance.	☐	☐	☐	☐	☐	☐
Regulatory/Compliance Knowledge: I highlighted knowledge of regulatory guidelines and compliance standards relevant to the role.	☐	☐	☐	☐	☐	☐
Relationship Building: I highlighted my experience in building and maintaining professional relationships both internally and externally.	☐	☐	☐	☐	☐	☐

MSL JOB APPLICATION TRACKING & INTERVIEW SELF-EVALUATION JOURNAL

INTERVIEW SELF-EVALUATION

3rd INTERVIEW

	Strongly Agree	Agree	Neutral	Disagree	Strongly Disagree	Not Applicable
Coachability: I demonstrated an openness to feedback and a willingness to incorporate suggestions provided by colleagues and management.	☐	☐	☐	☐	☐	☐
Clinical Data Interpretation: I demonstrated the ability to interpret and discuss clinical data effectively.	☐	☐	☐	☐	☐	☐
Flexibility: I demonstrated flexibility and adaptability in responding to unexpected questions or situations.	☐	☐	☐	☐	☐	☐
Overall Confidence: I felt confident and poised throughout the interview.	☐	☐	☐	☐	☐	☐
Handling Challenging Questions: I effectively navigated and responded to challenging or unexpected questions during the interview.	☐	☐	☐	☐	☐	☐
Succinct Responses to Interview Questions: I responded succinctly to interview questions, providing clear and concise answers without unnecessary elaboration.	☐	☐	☐	☐	☐	☐
Competitor Knowledge: I demonstrated knowledge of the competitive landscape and effectively communicated distinctions between the company's products and its competitors.	☐	☐	☐	☐	☐	☐

www.themslbook.com

MSL JOB APPLICATION TRACKING & INTERVIEW SELF-EVALUATION JOURNAL

INTERVIEW SELF-EVALUATION

3rd INTERVIEW

	Strongly Agree	Agree	Neutral	Disagree	Strongly Disagree	Not Applicable
Strategic Thinking: I demonstrated strategic thinking in discussing how the company's products fit into the broader healthcare landscape.	☐	☐	☐	☐	☐	☐
Digital Communication Skills: I effectively conveyed my proficiency in utilizing digital communication tools for scientific engagement.	☐	☐	☐	☐	☐	☐
Continual Learning: I highlighted my commitment to continual learning and staying updated on advancements in the therapeutic area.	☐	☐	☐	☐	☐	☐
Team Collaboration: I emphasized my ability to collaborate effectively with team members and cross-functional teams.	☐	☐	☐	☐	☐	☐
Enthusiasm for the Role: I effectively conveyed genuine enthusiasm for the role and the science of the product.	☐	☐	☐	☐	☐	☐
Asking Relevant Questions: I proactively asked relevant questions during the interview, demonstrating a genuine interest and understanding of the role.	☐	☐	☐	☐	☐	☐
STAR Method Application: When expected, I effectively utilized the STAR (Situation, Task, Action, Result) method when responding to behavioral questions.	☐	☐	☐	☐	☐	☐

MSL JOB APPLICATION TRACKING & INTERVIEW SELF-EVALUATION JOURNAL

3rd INTERVIEW

PRESENTATION SELF-EVALUATION*

	Strongly Agree	Agree	Neutral	Disagree	Strongly Disagree
Clarity of Message: I clearly and effectively communicated the key points of my presentation.	☐	☐	☐	☐	☐
Engagement with Audience: I maintained audience engagement by using effective visuals, body language, and vocal tone.	☐	☐	☐	☐	☐
Knowledge Demonstration: I demonstrated a comprehensive understanding of the subject matter and responded confidently to questions.	☐	☐	☐	☐	☐
Visual Aids Effectiveness: The visual aids (slides, charts, etc.) I utilized enhanced the overall impact of my presentation.	☐	☐	☐	☐	☐
Time Management: I effectively utilized the allotted time, ensuring all key points were covered within the specified timeframe.	☐	☐	☐	☐	☐
Adaptability to Audience: I adapted my presentation style to suit the needs and level of understanding of the audience.	☐	☐	☐	☐	☐
Overall Confidence: I felt confident and poised throughout the presentation.	☐	☐	☐	☐	☐
Communicating Scientific Information: I demonstrated strong presentation skills in conveying scientific information to a diverse audience.	☐	☐	☐	☐	☐

*Although most applicants will be expected to deliver a presentation once during the interview process (typically during the in-person interview), it's important to be prepared to present at any point throughout the process.

MSL JOB APPLICATION TRACKING & INTERVIEW SELF-EVALUATION JOURNAL

THANK-YOU LETTER

Date Sent: _____/_____/_____

Individual's Name:

Email Address:

NOTES

_____
_____
_____
_____
_____
_____
_____
_____
_____
_____
_____
_____

MSL JOB APPLICATION TRACKING & INTERVIEW SELF-EVALUATION JOURNAL

INTERVIEW DETAILS

Position Applied For: Company:

INTERVIEW DATE, TIME, FORMAT

Scheduled Interview Date: _____/_____/_____

Scheduled Interview Time: ____ : ____ ☐ AM ☐ PM

☐ Phone Interview
☐ Virtual Interview
☐ In-Person Interview

Interviewer Details

Names and Titles of Interviewer(s):

1. _____
2. _____
3. _____
4. _____
5. _____
6. _____

What I Did Well

_____
_____
_____
_____

What I Can Improve

_____
_____
_____
_____

MSL JOB APPLICATION TRACKING & INTERVIEW SELF-EVALUATION JOURNAL

4th INTERVIEW

INTERVIEW QUESTIONS

Which questions were most challenging to answer?

1. _____
2. _____
3. _____
4. _____

Key questions you were asked:

1. _____
2. _____
3. _____
4. _____

Self-assessment of my responses:

1. _____
2. _____
3. _____
4. _____

MSL JOB APPLICATION TRACKING & INTERVIEW SELF-EVALUATION JOURNAL

INTERVIEW SELF-EVALUATION

	Strongly Agree	Agree	Neutral	Disagree	Strongly Disagree	Not Applicable
Disease State / Therapeutic Area Expertise: I effectively communicated my expertise in the specific disease state and therapeutic area relevant to the role.	☐	☐	☐	☐	☐	☐
KOL Engagement: I effectively communicated my experience engaging Key Opinion Leaders (KOLs) and Health Care Providers (HCPs).	☐	☐	☐	☐	☐	☐
Product Knowledge: I demonstrated a deep understanding of the company's products and their clinical applications.	☐	☐	☐	☐	☐	☐
Clinical Trial Knowledge: I demonstrated a solid understanding of clinical trial methodologies and their relevance.	☐	☐	☐	☐	☐	☐
Regulatory/Compliance Knowledge: I highlighted knowledge of regulatory guidelines and compliance standards relevant to the role.	☐	☐	☐	☐	☐	☐
Relationship Building: I highlighted my experience in building and maintaining professional relationships both internally and externally.	☐	☐	☐	☐	☐	☐

MSL JOB APPLICATION TRACKING & INTERVIEW SELF-EVALUATION JOURNAL

4th INTERVIEW

INTERVIEW SELF-EVALUATION

	Strongly Agree	Agree	Neutral	Disagree	Strongly Disagree	Not Applicable
Coachability: I demonstrated an openness to feedback and a willingness to incorporate suggestions provided by colleagues and management.	☐	☐	☐	☐	☐	☐
Clinical Data Interpretation: I demonstrated the ability to interpret and discuss clinical data effectively.	☐	☐	☐	☐	☐	☐
Flexibility: I demonstrated flexibility and adaptability in responding to unexpected questions or situations.	☐	☐	☐	☐	☐	☐
Overall Confidence: I felt confident and poised throughout the interview.	☐	☐	☐	☐	☐	☐
Handling Challenging Questions: I effectively navigated and responded to challenging or unexpected questions during the interview.	☐	☐	☐	☐	☐	☐
Succinct Responses to Interview Questions: I responded succinctly to interview questions, providing clear and concise answers without unnecessary elaboration.	☐	☐	☐	☐	☐	☐
Competitor Knowledge: I demonstrated knowledge of the competitive landscape and effectively communicated distinctions between the company's products and its competitors.	☐	☐	☐	☐	☐	☐

MSL JOB APPLICATION TRACKING & INTERVIEW SELF-EVALUATION JOURNAL

4th INTERVIEW

INTERVIEW SELF-EVALUATION

	Strongly Agree	Agree	Neutral	Disagree	Strongly Disagree	Not Applicable
Strategic Thinking: I demonstrated strategic thinking in discussing how the company's products fit into the broader healthcare landscape.	☐	☐	☐	☐	☐	☐
Digital Communication Skills: I effectively conveyed my proficiency in utilizing digital communication tools for scientific engagement.	☐	☐	☐	☐	☐	☐
Continual Learning: I highlighted my commitment to continual learning and staying updated on advancements in the therapeutic area.	☐	☐	☐	☐	☐	☐
Team Collaboration: I emphasized my ability to collaborate effectively with team members and cross-functional teams.	☐	☐	☐	☐	☐	☐
Enthusiasm for the Role: I effectively conveyed genuine enthusiasm for the role and the science of the product.	☐	☐	☐	☐	☐	☐
Asking Relevant Questions: I proactively asked relevant questions during the interview, demonstrating a genuine interest and understanding of the role.	☐	☐	☐	☐	☐	☐
STAR Method Application: When expected, I effectively utilized the STAR (Situation, Task, Action, Result) method when responding to behavioral questions.	☐	☐	☐	☐	☐	☐

MSL JOB APPLICATION TRACKING & INTERVIEW SELF-EVALUATION JOURNAL

PRESENTATION SELF-EVALUATION*

4th INTERVIEW

	Strongly Agree	Agree	Neutral	Disagree	Strongly Disagree
Clarity of Message: I clearly and effectively communicated the key points of my presentation.	☐	☐	☐	☐	☐
Engagement with Audience: I maintained audience engagement by using effective visuals, body language, and vocal tone.	☐	☐	☐	☐	☐
Knowledge Demonstration: I demonstrated a comprehensive understanding of the subject matter and responded confidently to questions.	☐	☐	☐	☐	☐
Visual Aids Effectiveness: The visual aids (slides, charts, etc.) I utilized enhanced the overall impact of my presentation.	☐	☐	☐	☐	☐
Time Management: I effectively utilized the allotted time, ensuring all key points were covered within the specified timeframe.	☐	☐	☐	☐	☐
Adaptability to Audience: I adapted my presentation style to suit the needs and level of understanding of the audience.	☐	☐	☐	☐	☐
Overall Confidence: I felt confident and poised throughout the presentation.	☐	☐	☐	☐	☐
Communicating Scientific Information: I demonstrated strong presentation skills in conveying scientific information to a diverse audience.	☐	☐	☐	☐	☐

*Although most applicants will be expected to deliver a presentation once during the interview process (typically during the in-person interview), it's important to be prepared to present at any point throughout the process.

MSL JOB APPLICATION TRACKING & INTERVIEW SELF-EVALUATION JOURNAL

4th
INTERVIEW

THANK-YOU LETTER

Date Sent: _____/_____/_____

Individual's Name:

Email Address:

NOTES

_____
_____
_____
_____
_____
_____
_____
_____
_____
_____

www.ingramcontent.com/pod-product-compliance
Lightning Source LLC
Chambersburg PA
CBHW060424010526
44118CB00017B/2351